UBIK:
THE SCREENPLAY

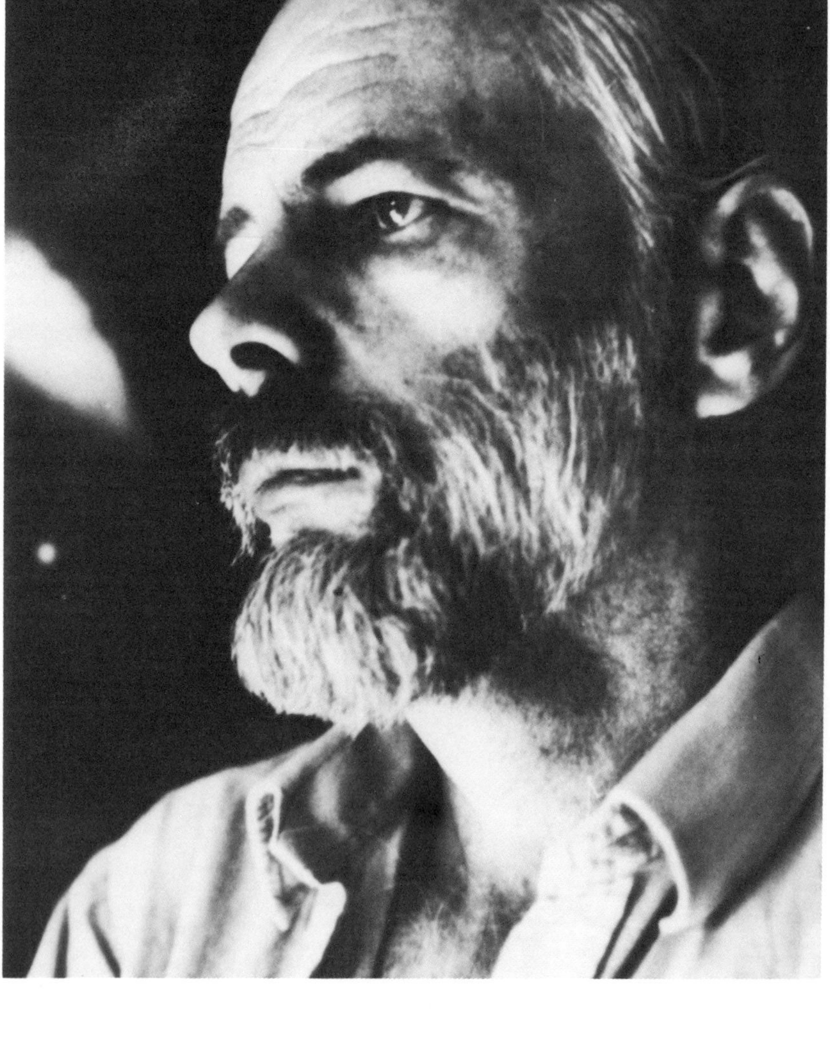

Ubik
THE SCREENPLAY

Philip K. Dick

Corroboree Press
Minneapolis, Minnesota
1985

UBIK: THE SCREENPLAY

First Edition
June 1985

Published by:
CORROBOREE PRESS
2729 Bloomington Avenue South
Minneapolis, Minnesota 55407

Copyright © 1985 by the estate of Philip K. Dick

Introduction © 1985 by Paul Williams
Foreword © 1985 by Tim Powers
Color Illustrations © 1985 by Doug Rice
Black and white illustrations and endpapers © 1985
by Val Lakey-Lindahn and Ron Lindahn

All rights reserved. No part of this book may be reproduced in any form or by any electronic or mechanical means including information storage and retrieval systems without explicit permission in writing from the Author's Estate or the Author's agent, except by a reviewer who may quote brief passages in a review to be printed in a magazine or newspaper, or electronically transmitted on radio or television. For information address Author's agent: Scott Meredith Literary Agency, Inc., 845 Third Avenue, New York, NY, 10022

Special edition ISBN 0-911169-07-5
Trade edition ISBN 0-911169-06-7
Library of Congress Catalog Card Number: 85-70137

For information about the Philip K. Dick Society, write to the Society at Box 611, Glen Ellen, California, 95442

Introduction

> Did you know that *UBIK* is true, and we're in a sort of cave, like Plato said, and they're showing us endless funky films; and now and then reality breaks through, as in *UBIK*, from our friend who was here once and then died?
> — Philip K. Dick, in a letter to Paul Williams, September 1974.

In late August of 1974, Philip K. Dick received a letter from Jean-Pierre Gorin, a French director who had worked with Jean-Luc Godard, saying he has had an offer to do a film and he wants it to be *UBIK*. Gorin described himself as "one of the great admirers of your work" and said "I made this trip to California just to see you and to discuss with you the whole project." One can imagine Dick's excitement. Within a few weeks Dick and Gorin met, at Dick's apartment in Fullerton, and Gorin made an arrangement with Dick for him to write a screenplay based on his novel.

Dick had never written a screenplay before (he did a few radio scripts in the 1950s, and wrote — on spec — a plot outline for an episode of the television drama "The Invaders"). But apparently Gorin's enthusiasm, and some money up front (with

Introduction

$2,500.00 more to come on delivery of a completed draft), overcame any qualms Dick may have had about moving into an unfamiliar medium. He sat down at the typewriter and started his screenplay sometime in late September, 1974, and, faced with a three-month deadline, finished it instead in three weeks (Dick has been known to write novels, sometimes very good ones, in similar spans of time). By mid-October PKD had proudly delivered his completed manuscript and was waiting for the promised payment.

Payment never came, alas; Gorin complained first of a liver ailment and then of loss of enthusiasm on the part of his backers, and ultimately vanished from the scene. The movie never got made. (But never say die. Fourteen years elapsed between the first option deal on *Do Androids Dream of Electric Sheep?* and the eventual completion and release of "BLADE RUNNER.")

In any event, Dick had some fun before the episode ran its course. He wrote to the actress Kay Lenz (and maybe also to Victoria Principal), suggesting she would be perfect to play the part of Pat Conley in the movie. He wrote to a friend about a visit from Gorin and one of his prospective backers in which the "money-man" said, "You know, *Ubik* is a lot like the *I Ching*."

> To them, I suggested the following, as a means of contacting Ubik or God or whatever; you buy a box of that breakfast cereal in the form of edible letters (semi-edible), and then after you pour milk on your little plastic bowl of them you watch and see which letters swim up to the surface to form what words. They had to admit that as a way of contacting God and getting His message, I had managed to put my finger on (or spoon into) *the* link between the antique methods and the plastic new. "Would make a great scene in the movie," they said. Maybe it would.

But the most fun Dick had was writing the screenplay itself. I visited him at the end of October, 1974, to interview him for an article in *Rolling Stone*. He was very pleased with the screenplay, which he'd just finished, and shared with me some of the insights into his own works that he'd had as a result of "reliving" one of his own novels, translating it into a new medium, making the leap from story told in words that convey images to story told in images that speak words. It gave him a sense of the dynamic of his own storytelling process, a sense both affectionate and eerie of how real his characters and situations are to him as he writes about them. He reported, in fact, that he had been having dreams throughout the summer of 1974 that he realized, once he reread the novel in order to write the screenplay, were actually scenes from *UBIK*. This was before he got the screenplay assignment. It was almost like Runciter was trying to break through and contact *him*.

Here are some relevant transcripts from my conversations with Philip K. Dick at the end of October, 1974:

PKD: When I was doing the screenplay, I realized that I've got a little screen in my head, and the people walk around on it.
PW: They're real.
PKD: They're *little*, Paul, they're about that big (laughter). They move around, y'know, and I was going like this, looking up, typing, and saying, "and there goes Joe out the door, slam!" I didn't realize it until I did the screenplay, where I had to visualize, and I realized I didn't have to 'cause I was, I didn't know any other way to do it. And I got to going, I was literally looking up, type type type and look up. ...With one character [from a book-in-progress, not the screenplay] I deduced he had a child 'cause I could see a tricycle in the driveway.

PKD: Let me tell you a strange thing. It is perfectly conceivable to me that in moments of crisis I could consult Leo Bulero or Runciter, as the Greeks used to consult the Delphic Oracle.
PW: How would you do it? What process would you use?
PKD: Written form. I'd put myself in there, third person. Ah... "He walked into the office. 'Glen,' he said to Runciter, 'Could I have a few minutes of your time? I've got a problem here I can't handle.' Runciter glanced up..." and so on. And, "'Glen, the problem is as follows. What do you think I should do?'" Then actually I could gain from Runciter's responses things which I could never extract from sheer...Runciter would say something that I would never think of. ...This whole thing is a very strange business. Like, just having done this screenplay, Runciter and Joe Chip became so real to me that I can imagine writing about them forever, and they'd always say new things. But they would evolve, I imagine, under those circumstances. And I would learn from what they said. Okay, now where was this wisdom before I wrote it down? Was it in my head? No, it really wasn't — didn't take place until, you know, the deed. As Goethe's Faust said, "In the beginning was the word? No. In the beginning was the deed." This occurs in the deed, the act of writing. These things occur when you write. Not thinking.

PKD: ...I had a funny experience I'd never had before, in that regard. Before I did the screenplay, before I knew I was going to be doing the screenplay, before Jean-Pierre wrote to me. I had these dreams, in which I was somebody else. I know I wasn't myself. For one thing, I went in the kitchen and talked to my mother and it wasn't my mother, it was somebody else entirely. I noticed that when I got up my wallet had a great deal of money in it and the bills were arranged differently than I arrange them. And I began to grasp the fact that my friends were a different set of people and when I woke up I thought, that's strange, I was inside that person looking out. And then later when I was doing the screenplay I discovered scenes in the novel which I had dreamed. And I

Introduction

was dreaming from the standpoint of some of the characters in the novel. For instance, I dreamed that scene in the book where Al Hammond takes out — well, let's put it the other way. I dreamed that I was taking out my wallet and giving some money to a kind of a nitwit guy who had to take a drive to go to a funeral. And I was giving him some bills. And I'm reading *UBIK*, and there's this scene where Al Hammond gets out his wallet and gives Joe Chip some money, to pay for a hotel bill, and then of course Runciter's dead, and the funeral is coming up soon... The similarity was too great to ignore. But I hadn't read *UBIK* for years, and I didn't know at the time I had the dream that I was going to be doing the screenplay. And I find that very strange.

Now of course when I wrote the screenplay it made it very easy for me to write those scenes, because I had already been through... I found in fact dream after dream that I had had were scenes from *UBIK*. But they were meaningless when I had them, in relation to *UBIK* — although I did guess that they were related to *UBIK*, I did notice that it had something to do with *UBIK*, these dreams. Then after all this I get this letter from Jean-Pierre. But in the dreams, I'm characters in the novel, acting out scenes from the book. Damnedest thing. But it sure made writing the screenplay easy. But it made me wonder, you know, are these characters really real? Do I think I invent them, but in actual fact I am merely picking them up from somewhere?

I had the strange feeling that somehow this had really happened, in some way, as I did the screenplay; that I was describing things that actually had happened. I remember one dream I had. In the dream Tess and I were in the kitchen on a high stool, getting down a cereal box; and on the back of the cereal box is extremely valuable information, directed at us. And we were both reading it. The relationship between that and *UBIK* is an obvious one. And this kind of dream continued for months, where written information like that was directed to me. That's exactly how Runciter communicated to Joe Chip, was on the backs of cereal boxes.

Now, if I had known I was going to be doing a screenplay of *UBIK*, or was in process — but at that point I had no idea I'd ever be... I can't account for that, except for I am absolutely sure that in *UBIK* I touched upon, as Lem says, something that is real but we've lost track of it. He said, "resurrected a sacerdotal power," something like that, "that has been buried for aeons." He said something about trash containing valuable things within it. I don't know what he means. I wrote *UBIK* in '68...this is '74, and suddenly I began to dream these dreams in which cereal boxes, labels, are addressed to me; and a few months later, four months later, I'm suddenly commissioned to write a screenplay of *UBIK*. And I find to my amazement that half the dreams I've had during the previous four to six months are relevant to scenes I will be writing into the screenplay. And then they go right into the screenplay. So that's how come I could do it in three weeks. It was all there, it was all there before I heard from Jean-Pierre.

PW: How did your breakdowns affect your writing?

PKD: It gave me sympathy for my characters. I could never mock my characters, for screwing up, especially. I was dedicated thereupon to characters who, when walking out the door, would fall over the front step on their nose, and I could never mock them for it. I never felt superior to my characters, after screwing up myself. A guy who can't even pay his front door to open, like Joe Chip — I had completely fucked up my life, I was completely incompetent, and I loved my characters for their incompetence. Also it made me need my characters more.

Reading Philip K. Dick's screenplay of *UBIK* is like going with the author on a guided tour of his own book, waving his pointer at beloved absurdities and little pivotal moments when you can actually see the vitality ebb out of the landscape, wise-cracking all the time, leering at the attractive female characters and bemoaning their power over him even though he created them and determines their actions. In no sense is this the rendering of a cool technician. It's hot, all the time—the situation is alive—even when it makes no sense, it carries with it the conviction of that which is actual, like right in front of your nose. "Runciter and Joe Chip became so real to me I can imagine writing about them forever." The answer to Dick's perennial "What is real?" is, Runciter and Joe Chip are real. Not real like true-to-life, accurate representations of something—real like palpable, like they exist. Dick in the passion of telling a story was more certain of his characters' reality than of his friends' or wives' or children's. Or his own. What's real is these people and their immediate crises. To read this screenplay is in some sense to walk in Dick's reality with him, and see it through his eyes. Or to wallow in it, to roll around in it, to laugh and kick and flail one's arms.

After the screenplay was completed, the characters began to recede again. ("What matters to me is the *writing*, the act of manufacturing the novels, because while I am doing it, at that particular moment, I am in the world I'm writing about. It is real to me, completely and utterly. Then, when I'm finished, and have to stop, withdraw from that world *forever*—that destroys me. The men and women have ceased talking. They no longer move. I'm alone...Where is Mr. Tagomi, the protagonist in *The Man in the High Castle*? He has left me; we are cut off from each other. To read the novel does not restore Mr. Tagomi, place him once again where I can hear him talk... My friends are dead, and as much as I love my wife, daughter, cat—none of these nor all of these are enough. The vacuum is terrible. Don't write for a living; sell shoelaces. Don't let it happen to you." —PKD, "Notes Made Late at Night by a Weary SF Writer," written 1968, perhaps shortly after finishing *UBIK*, the novel.) What took their place in Phil's consciousness, judging from his correspondence, was speculation about the ideas, the concepts, the uncovered

Introduction

cosmic truths expressed in *UBIK*. A palpable impact of PKD's episode with writing the screenplay was to embed *UBIK* and its concepts into his hundreds of thousands of philosophical and theological speculation, his Exegesis, written in longhand and sometimes in letters to friends from 1974 to 1982. The Exegesis centers around or constantly returns to Dick's mystical experience(s) in March 1974; his involvement with dreaming, retelling, reliving *UBIK* in the summer and fall of the same year seems to be the source of a major subtheme, along with a variety of odd events connected with his novel *Flow My Tears, the Policeman Said*.

By way of example, here is an undated fragment, believed to be from late 1974, possibly even written while Dick was working on the screenplay, but more probably sometime in the month or two following:

> In *UBIK* the forward moving force of time (or time-force expressed as an ergic field) has ceased. All changes result from that. Forms regress. The substrate is revealed. Cooling (entropy) is allowed to set in unimpeded. Equilibrium is affected by the vanishing of the forward-moving time force field. The bare bones, so to speak, of the world, our world, are revealed. We see the Logos addressing the many living entities. Assisting and advising them. We are now aware of the Atman everywhere. The press of time on everything, having been abolished, reveals many elements underlying our phenomena.
> If time stops, this is what takes place, these changes.
> Not frozen-ness, but revelation.
> There are still the retrograde forces remaining, at work. And also underlying prositive forces other than time. The disappearance of the force-field we call time reveals both good and bad things; which is to say, coaching entities (Runciter, who is the Logos), the Atman (Ubik), Ella; it isn't a static world but it begins to *cool*. What is missing is a form of heat: the Aton. The Logos (Runciter) can tell you *what* to do, but you lack the energy—heat, force—to do it. (i.e. time.)

The fragment continues, at some length. When Dick's characters depart, the novel or screenplay or story finished, he consoles himself by talking to himself. He could talk to himself on paper to the tune of fifty or a hundred handwritten pages in an evening. He also liked to write letters. On December 28, 1974, he wrote to an acquaintance:

> Thank you in particular for what you said about *UBIK*. Just the other day I looked up the Greek philosopher Empedocles and I was amazed to see that *UBIK* in many ways expresses his world-view. It is a view generally discarded these days. In May of this year a guy from France doing his doctoral thesis on

UBIK flew here and asked me, "You know Empedocles?" to which I had to admit, no, I didn't even know the name. The French guy got very angry, as if he believed I was lying, and walked out. Now I can see why. It is impossible to believe that anyone could write *UBIK* without having gotten the concepts from Empedocles. By the way — Empedocles, I read, believed that he would be reincarnated and return some day. I'm not kidding. He expected to come back...But I bet he didn't anticipate finding himself in Fullerton. I guess the part where they're all dead is because ol' E. has been dead these many centuries and knows a lot about how it feels (I wish I was kidding when I say all this, but I'm not; I mean, I really sort of believe this).

The final word, in this little trip through Philip-K.-Dick-land, belongs appropriately to Joe Chip, from the screenplay:

Perhaps this verifies an ancient philosophy: Plato's ideal objects, the universals which in each class are real. Prior forms must carry on an invisible, residual life in every object. The past is latent, submerged, but still here, capable of rising to the surface once the later printing, through some unfortunate accident, vanishes. The man contains — not the boy — but earlier men. But didn't Plato think that something survived the decay and decline of forms? Something inside, not able to decay? The body ending, like Wendy did, and the soul — out of its nest the bird, flown elsewhere. To be reborn again, as the Tibetan Book of the Dead says. It really is true. Christ, I hope so. Because then we can all meet again. As in Winnie-the-Pooh, in another part of the forest...

Paul Williams
Glen Ellen, California
February 1985

Foreword

In 1968, '69, and '70, Philip K. Dick published four powerful and oddly disturbing novels—*Do Androids Dream of Electric Sheep?, Galactic Pot-Healer, Ubik* and *A Maze of Death.* In retrospect it's easy to see that their backhandedly numinous qualities are a consequence of being based on theological questions, and that this new direction was to culminate in such authoritative masterworks as *Valis* and *The Transmigration of Timothy Archer;* but in these four earlier novels the theological element is tentative and not-yet-consistent, and Dick goes out of his way, almost with an air of self-consciousness, to conceal it behind some of the most entertainingly exaggerated grotesquerie the science fiction field has ever come up with. And since Dick's characters are at the same time as complex and convincing here as they ever were, the dialogue, conflicts and "logic" lure us into a sort of Moebius-strip-tease show, and leave us feeling as if we'd been rotated through some hitherto-unsuspected literary dimension and now don't fit into the world quite as well as we did before.

Like Bob Dylan song lyrics or Bassho haiku or boxing matches between men and kangaroos, these novels resist being rendered down to reveal any solid, clearly-intended themes; rather than seeming to be the result of painstaking architectural construction, they give the impression of "purest eye-to-hand first-draft mastery," as Thomas Disch has noted. So in this *UBIK* screenplay we have a couple of things Dick rarely gave us—a story reconsidered, and one presented more directly than could be done from within the novel form. Film is a more intrusive medium, and *UBIK* is certainly made of intrusions; at one point Dick considered having the movie end with the film itself appearing to undergo a series of reversions: to black-and-white, then to the awkward jerkiness of very early movies, then to a crookedly-jammed frame which proceeds to blacken, bubble and melt away, leaving only the white glare of the projection bulb, which in turn deteriorates to leave the theater in darkness, and might almost leave the moviegoer wondering what sort of dilapidated, antique jalopy he'll find his car-keys fitting when he goes outside.

Since Dick had at least two important experiences between 1969, when the novel *UBIK* was published, and October of '74, when this screenplay was written—the "in the street" period that forms the basis of *A Scanner Darkly*, and the mystical visions that lead to *Valis*—we might expect these experiences to be reflected in this "re-write" of *UBIK*.

They're not, though. *UBIK* seems to have been too perfect a vehicle for Dick's feelings in the late '60s to serve comfortably for those of the mid-'70s. I think the Aphrodite-like naked torso in the Ubik bra ad derives from the mystical experiences, and I think that when Joe Chip says,

"You know, things can happen to you so much worse than you ever anticipated. Worse than your worst anxieties. The universe can think up far worse things than your own mind."

it's the survivor of *A Scanner Darkly* speaking. But the real value of this screenplay lies elsewhere.

Dick included far more parenthetical description and interpretation than can be standard for screenplays, and so we have here his considered, after-the-fact portraits of Glen Runciter, Ella Runciter, Joe Chip, Pat Conley, and Ubik itself. And too, with a facility that's scarce among novelists, he smoothly adapts his story to the wider, deeper ranges of the film medium. The Ubik "ads" are much more effective as actual intrusions than as chapter head-

Foreword

ings, the soundtrack becomes a central element (and makes us wonder what music Dick would have chosen to compliment some of his other novels), and he presents the dysfunctions in time and perception even more effectively when he imagines them enacted on a movie screen. In some ways, in fact, it almost seems as though we're getting a purer version of *UBIK* — something closer to the original conception than the text of the novel.

UBIK has been optioned for movie production at least once, and I remember Dick telling me one time that he had sent a copy of the novel to the agent of Victoria Principal — whom he revered — in hopes that she'd wind up reading it. (He'd written his telephone number, and a plea that she call him, on one of the middle pages. She never did call.) A fine movie could certainly be made of *UBIK*, but even if this screenplay is never produced and the movie remains just something for us to imagine, this text will be treasured as a look at the *UBIK* events and characters from a more direct viewpoint — from a seat, as it were, at least several rows closer to the stage.

Tim Powers
La Mirada, California
February 1985

UBIK:
THE SCREENPLAY

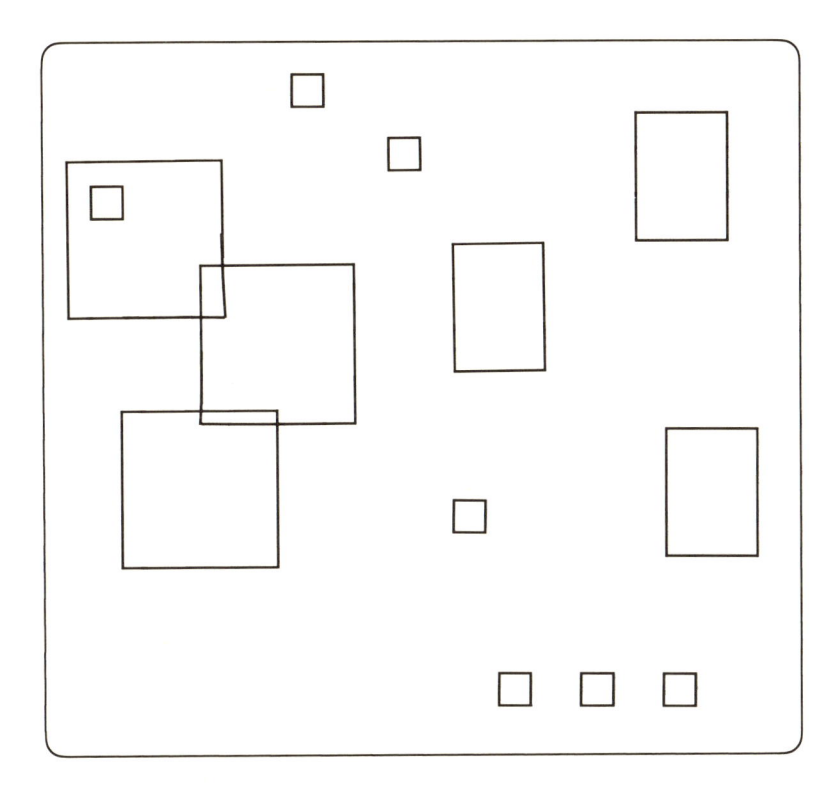

1.

Fade in. Changing pattern of colored lights like futuristic Christmas display, but with radar-screen concentric circles superimposed. It fills screen like an abstract but constantly fluctuating graphic. Then we see three people unblinkingly scrutinizing it, holding clipboards and making notes. Behind them in modern letters on wall, the mysterious initials: R.A. The three people remind us of the witches who open MacBeth, except that all are men. It's evident from their professionally relaxed posture that they've been there a long time. Their clothing is not like ours, but not the "Star Trek" control room uniforms of SF films; the BLOND MAN wears a dark velvet shirt and yellow slacks, the BALD MAN wears a bright crepe shirt with ruffled sleeves, the SLENDER MAN wears a casual work smock with the same initials R.A. stitched on the bosom. The room is medium sized. We hear equipment whirring. The positions of the lights alter unceasingly; every so often one of the three men points with a pen, or nods with his head, toward a particular colored light which has shifted its location. Now and then their lips move as the three men discuss what they see, but we hear nothing because of the constant electronic background. We and the three men notice more and more one green light moving from left to right. Then abruptly the light disappears; a gong-like sound, not loud, is heard, but all three start visibly.

BLOND MAN: S. Dole Melipone.

The SLENDER MAN *picks up modernistic telephone which has viewscreen on it, sticks punchcard into it, holds receiver to his ear.*

SLENDER MAN: S. Dole Melipone.

On viewscreen of phone a distorted face appears, cloudy, as if swimming from a dream; fisheye lens makes it clown-like, absurd. The man is asleep, now waking as if being born; he is in his fifties with rumpled gray hair, double-chin, but impressive, heavy-set but not fat; rather, he is powerfully built, a Romanesque face, a leader. Even roused from sleep he can glare commandingly. This is shown by the speed at which he grasps what's being said. This is GLEN RUNCITER.

RUNCITER: Where is he?

SLENDER MAN: S. Dole Melipone is gone, Mr. Runciter. Off the map board.

RUNCITER: Well, did you look behind the mapboard? On the floor?

SLENDER MAN: Edie Dorn and two other inertials followed him to a motel named the Bonds of Erotic Polymorphic Experience, a sixty-unit subsurface structure catering to businessmen and their hookers who don't want to be entertained. To be on the safe side we had one of our own telepaths, Mr. G. G. Ashwood, go in and read him. Ashwood found a scramble pattern surrounding Melipone's mind, so he couldn't catch anything clear. He therefore went back to Topeka, Kansas, where he's currently scouting a new employee possibility. That can wait though, I'm sure.

By now RUNCITER, *on viewscreen, is fully awake and calm.*

RUNCITER: Maybe it wasn't Melipone.

Taking phone from the SLENDER MAN, *the* BALD MAN *speaks.*

BALD MAN: We requested Joe Chip to go in there and run tests on the magnitude and minitude of the field being generated there at the Bonds of Erotic Polymorphic Experience Motel. Chip says it registered, at its height, 68.2 B.L.R. units of telepathic aura, which only Melipone, among all the known telepaths,

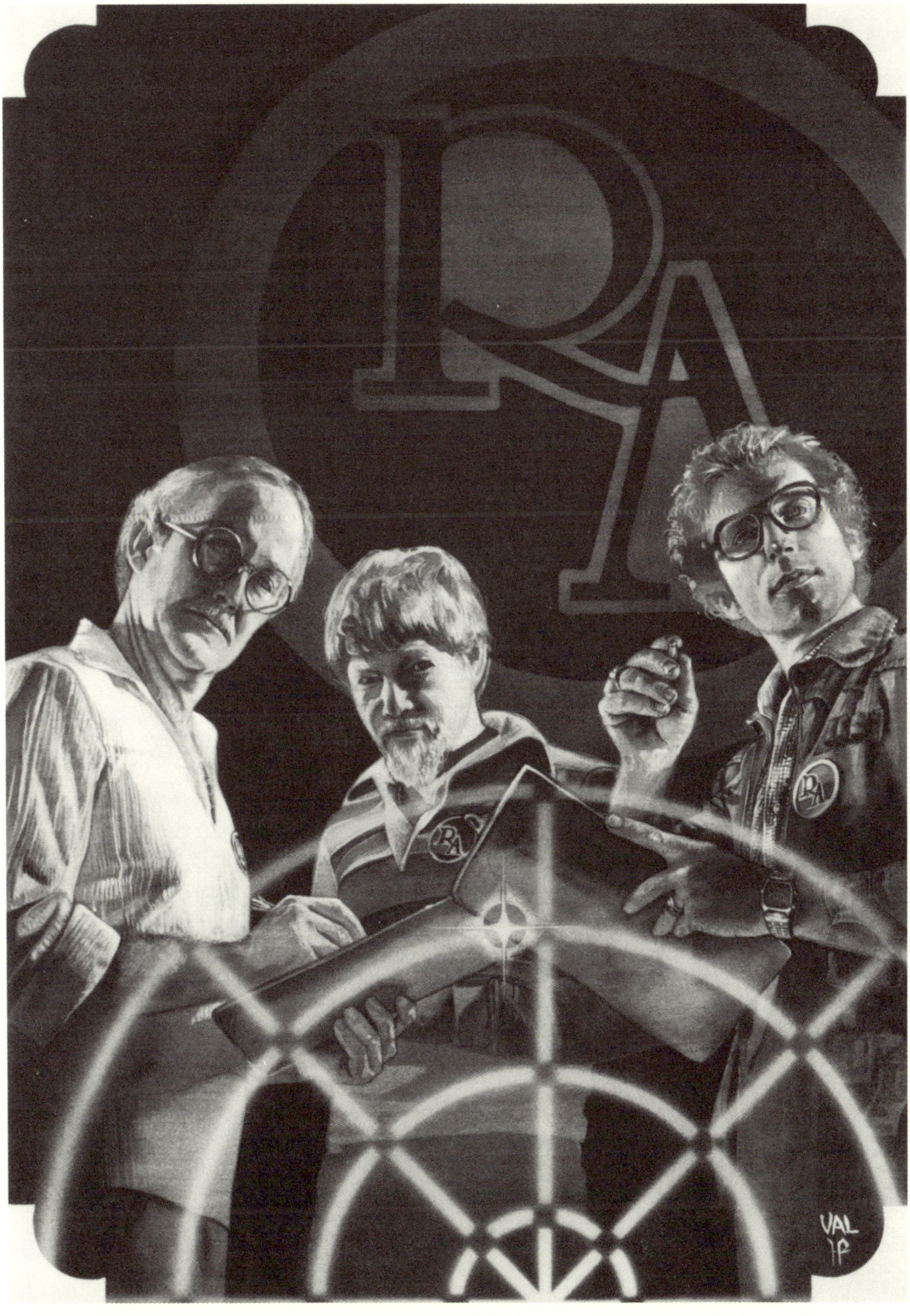
VAL

can produce.

A pause in which all four men are silent, evidently thinking. All, including the small electronic viewscreen face of RUNCITER, *are grim.*

RUNCITER: Okay . . . I'll consult my dead wife.

The three others show no particular reaction; none move; the electronic background sounds continue. Fade out.

2.

This is the title sequence. Titles will superimpose over detailing of scene: sudden cut to razzle-dazzle gingerbread baroque plastic and tinsel building like combination Mormon Temple and California drive-in, with vast parking area, garish tinted fountains, shrubs cut into bizarre shapes, benches and what appear to be combination small shrines and soft-drink dispensing machines. People roam along walks, unusually solemnly and slowly. There are stuffed animals which move when approached, rigidly and mechanically, giving the entire structure, including the people themselves, an oddly artificial appearance. This is the Beloved Brethren Moratorium; like a fair it has a certain festive manner, but the audible music is Beethoven's "Missa Solemnis," in stark contrast to the strolling people in varicolored clothing. The music conveys death to us; the visual scene, life.

The music is not at background level and it intrudes abruptly: the "Gloria" section. The visual colors are tints; the women seem to wear long light pastel skirts; some carry parasols, giving it an almost old-fashioned quality, a leisurely pace. Gradual change of camera angle reveals the entrance with the Beloved Brethren Moratorium sign over the church-like doors; the sign, unexpectedly, is sedate and in a medieval style: in high taste—and yet the total effect of the scene is as if Disneyland had a Cathedral-land section, a recreation, a simulation for the purpose of bringing tourists and money. When the camera pans, however, the faces of the people are appropriately somber, despite their gay attire. The only true joy is shown on the face of a small child pursuing a white duck—which turns out to be on wheels as it hurries off. It is fake.

3.

Interior of Beloved Brethren Moratorium, which is more like our contemporary hospital interior: corridors and lounges. The Bee-

UBIK: The Screenplay

thoven music is still heard, but from speakers which the characters also hear. It is at background. Along comes a sweet-faced, smiling young man, wearing make-up, knickers and a gray sweatshirt with the portrait of J.S. Bach printed on it. This is the owner, HERBERT SCHOENHEIT VON VOGELSANG, *a fussy person. He does more managing in his head than he does in actuality, so problems are perpetually a little beyond his control. An elderly gentleman, walking uncertainly, approaches him. The conversation between* HERBERT *and the* ELDERLY GENTLEMAN *is hectic and rapid. We catch only bits and pieces of it, giving us only partial clues.*

ELDERLY GENTLEMAN: About eighty years old, very small and wizened. My grandmother.

HERBERT: Twill only be a moment, sir.

HERBERT *accepts plastic credit card from* ELDERLY GENTLEMAN, *goes back into cold-pac region of the moratorium, slamming door reading "Employees Only." Here lie transparent plastic caskets everywhere, in bins, as if this is the inventory of the place; unlike our present-day caskets, however, they resemble ships. Frost lies over them, and now* HERBERT's *breath is visible. Each casket bears a large elaborate code-number. Each, too, has electronic communications hardware attached: coils of covered wire, booster boxes, relay switches.* HERBERT *goes about searching to match the numbered credit card he holds with the correct casket. When he finds it he studies a medical-type chart, then lifts down a portable "protophason amplifier" from a storage hook on the wall and plugs it into the casket; the "protophason amplifier" is characterized by making the person within the casket audible, via a small speaker, to* HERBERT.

HALF-LIFER: . . . and then Tillie sprained her ankle and we never thought it'd heal; she was so giddy about it, wanting to start walking again immediately . . .

HALF-LIFER *drones on;* HERBERT *isn't listening to content, only checking a meter for volume level; seems satisfied and unplugs "protophason amplifier" unit, then nods curtly to uniformed moratorium technician, who comes forward.* HERBERT *returns to the posh part of the building where the customers are permitted, is assailed by several of them at once with similar requests about loved ones they wish to visit; each customer holds up the plastic numbered credit-type card, trying to attract his attention.*

ELDERLY GENTLEMAN: You checked her out, did you?

Philip K. Dick

HERBERT: Personally, sir. Functioning perfectly.

HERBERT *is overworked and hardpressed; tries to deal with the other waiting customers. His angelic look is becoming strained.*

HERBERT: Happy Resurrection Day, sir.

HERBERT *nods to one person after another; he adroitly moves on, comes to a large alcove in which customers sit with headphones on. They are visiting their loved ones who we saw in the caskets, in "half-life."*

PLUMP LADY: Flora, dear, can you hear me? I think I can hear you much better than the last time. (*Anxiously*) Do you suppose you could pull yourself together a little bit more, Flora, and stop dreaming and pay attention? You know, dear, the traffic is terrible and—

Voices of the various customers intermingle, all of this sort: anxious concern, peevishness, self-pity, devotion out of duty. HERBERT *makes good his escape into his office, where his rather attractive young female secretary sits "typing," which is to say, using futuristic transcribing machine: she merely places her fingers against a colored screen, and her thoughts are printed out at high speed.*

HERBERT: When I die—

SECRETARY: Yes, Herr Schoenheit von Vogelsang.

HERBERT: (*More relaxed now*) I'll stipulate that my heirs revive me one day per century. No more; just one day.

SECRETARY: But the high maintenance cost for them, Herr. They might—

HERBERT: Bury me?

SECRETARY: In the ground, Herr. Six feet under. With worms, Herr.

HERBERT: Burial is barbaric. Remnant of the primitive origins of our culture. Worms. Yes, there are worms down there. (*Mostly to himself*) I just listened to an old soul who's almost to her end; ah, the number is—well, anyhow, she rambled on. Frozen like a haddock and still rambling on, thinking about someone named Tillie and a sprained ankle. They do not know, some of them. They do not know. They think the world is still real. They—

Light flashes on his SECRETARY's *desk; she reaches, cocks her head and listens to an inaudible message;* HERBERT *pauses in his rambling.*

SECRETARY: (*Matter of factly*) An arrival, Herr, at the loading dock. VIP; they want you personally.

HERBERT: (*Still in rambling philosophical mood and not wanting to go back out into the hubbub of customers; he pauses at exit door*) Come with me and fill out the forms. *Ich bin mude.*

The SECRETARY *rises from her desk; we see that her midsection bulges: she is several months pregnant, yet pretty, with the warm flushed features and coloration of a pregnant young woman.*

HERBERT: What's in there?

SECRETARY: My little baby.

HERBERT: He is in half-life, too, so to speak.

SECRETARY: Yes, Herr.

HERBERT: (*Nosily*) *Du hast keinen Mann, nicht wahr?*

SECRETARY: No, Herr, I'm not married.

The light flashes on her desk again, urgently; both persons react by moving together from the office, their attention back to business.

HERBERT: I wonder about the protophason flow in 426-35-E, that banker who they come and revive every time the stock market dips. I think either he has had it or there is a short in the booster circuitry. He shouldn't be that weak. They've drained him almost out of it, of course, by using him so much. If I were him I'd feed them wrong advice and bankrupt them.

SECRETARY: But they are his family, Herr. His heirs.

HERBERT: (*Eying her*) I would like our technicians to hook up some sort of booster linkage to you someday and see what—

SECRETARY: Please do not mess around with my stomach, Herr. That is one of the nicest aspects of this job here, that nobody messes around with my stomach.

4.
Outside onto loading dock. Two men wearing uniforms marked "Atlas Interplan Van & Storage" are carefully trundling handtruck from futuristic airship in park position; strapped onto

Philip K. Dick

handtruck like refrigerator or other valuable new appliance is a nebulous human form in a plastic bag. Ice can be seen within. The two men move rapidly. Now uniformed employees of the moratorium appear to receive the dead man: for this is an inert corpse. One Atlas Interplan employee makes a notation on a clipboard, passes it to a moratorium employee, along with a pen, for him to sign in receipt. It is all done swiftly and expertly, but with no feeling; almost at once the newly arrived frozen corpse disappears aboard his handtruck into the moratorium building. HERBERT takes the clipboard and reads the sheet of information; his SECRETARY wanders over to the edge of the loading dock to stand with hands in the pockets of her apron-like maternity skirt, gazing meditatively out at the far-distant mountains, her duties forgotten; there she stands, pretty and pregnant, against the scenery of the unloading stage front and the hills in the background.

The camera moves back and new figure appears, approaching those on the loading dock. It is GLEN RUNCITER. They are unaware of him. He moves very slowly but inexorably, bearing down on HERBERT. It is a one-way view: RUNCITER, approaching them all, is aware of them with no reciprocal awareness, and we sense the advantage he has thereby. Already, he dominates the scene by this advantage. His approach to them is measured, deliberate and perceptive.

RUNCITER: Mr. Schoenheit von Vogelsang.

HERBERT *glances up a little irritably from his reading; seeing who it is, he is quick to adjust his expression to one of tact, even unctious welcome; the clipboard is forgotten. His lips move in greeting but we hear nothing, oddly.*

RUNCITER: How is Ella?

Still as if taken aback, there is no response from HERBERT. *The quite impressive sound of* RUNCITER's *voice has caused all the people on the loading dock to glance toward him.*

RUNCITER: Ready to be cranked up for a talk? She's only twenty years old; she ought to be in better shape than you or me. (*Chuckles*)

RUNCITER's *manner is that of an American, old-fashioned, fatherly captain-of-industry: personal rather than the cold and efficient manner which a more modern type such as* HERBERT *shows. He is a warm person, obviously, and betrays on his features his feelings; there is no mask, no transactional persona. He is one individual, one independent and unique human being, approaching another—approaching him and relating to him on that—the human—basis. And yet he is impressive and powerful; he dominates these other people, and they seem smaller than he, in the sense of less complete: partial persons—except for the* SECRETARY, *who stands apart, watching, her arms folded. He is also rather old, and although expensively dressed in a double-breasted plastic-and-silk suit, his hair is towsled.* RUNCITER *is not a handsome man, but he is someone to take seriously: as* HERBERT *obviously does. In short,* RUNCITER *is one of those rare and influential men whose wrong guesses in situations are usually better than the average man's correct ones. Or, at the very least, those wrong guesses—or hunches or impulses—are more colorful. More interesting. And certainly more unanticipated. And yet, despite this, we sense that* RUNCITER *somehow stays always in touch with common sense: with the real. It is this abiding quality of the genuine which is the most pronounced aspect of* RUNCITER; *whatever defects and faults he may have, he is never fake.*

HERBERT: You have not been here for some time, Mister Runciter.

RUNCITER: This is a moment of importance, von Vogelsang. We, my associates and myself, are in a line of business that surpasses all rational understanding. I'm not at liberty to make disclosures at this time, but we consider matters at present to be ominous but not, however, hopeless. Despair is not indicated—not by any means. Where is Ella?

HERBERT: I'll bring her from the bin to the consultation lounge for you. Do you have your numbered claim-check, Mister Runciter?

RUNCITER: God no. I lost it months ago. But you know who my wife is; you can find her. Ella Runciter, about twenty. Brown hair and eyes.

Glances around impatiently, then puts his hand on HERBERT's *shoulder to urge him into motion.*

Where did you put the lounge? It used to be located where I could find it.

HERBERT: (*To* SECRETARY) Show Mister Runciter to the consultation lounge. And see to it that he has privacy.

SECRETARY *moves toward Runciter. Dissolve.*

Philip K. Dick

5.

Pan up fade in; not the lounge but ELLA RUNCITER *lying face-up in cold-pac, face-up with arms slightly lifted toward her ears, frozen in two senses: frozen physically in ice and snow and mist, and frozen into immobility. Her mouth shows discomfort; it is somewhat open, as if this freeze-frame-like view of her shows her during an ordeal. Her eyes are open and staring, but the pupils are made opaque by the layer of frost which has built up—obviously over the years, as with an old and undefrosted refrigerator system. We sense she is somehow straining against cords which bind her; the half-raised arms, the concerned mouth, the air of unhappiness, of being troubled. The fact that she cannot move does not tell us that she is dead, because we see her straining, although unavailingly, against this rigidity, this frozen state. This is not a corpse, a dead person; this is a person frozen and alive.* ELLA *is not a body;* ELLA *is a person. Her torment, however, is of an anxious sort, rather than an indication of agony; it is as if some unseen matter perpetually concerns her. A matter which she cannot resolve. There is a slight, but visible, continual alteration of the frost partially obscuring her; this gives her a three-dimensional quality, as if a landscape. Although she cannot move, we see occasional drip-drips of water, a fogging up of the glass between us and her, and, as the camera pans back, we see chugging equipment attached to her boat-like transparent casket. Superimposed on this slightly altering scene is this audio track:*

RUNCITER: I can't talk to Ella in here. Not with all these people. Look, it's full. (*Pause*) Mister von Vogelsang, isn't there a more private sanctum sanctorum for confidential communications? What I have to discuss with Ella my wife is not a matter which we at Runciter Associates are ready at this particular time to reveal to the world.

HERBERT: I can make Mrs. Runciter available to you in one of our suites, sir. I can fully appreciate your apprehension regarding intimacy—

RUNCITER: (*Breaking in*) Privacy.

HERBERT: Yes, I meant privacy. You are—let me see—Runciter Associates is a . . . prudence organization? We had cause to hire a prudence organization here once, not too long ago. A telepath had infiltrated our staff, evidently to monitor conversations—possibly certain secret *specific* conversations—between half-lifers and their visitors. A scout from one of your anti-psi organizations picked up the telepathic field and had us notified at once. Like a termite inspector, you know, in an old-time wooden house. Alerts you to your peril and then (*Chuckles*) sprays them.

RUNCITER: (*Drily*) Nullifies them. Nullifies the field with a balancing inertial. Yes, this office will do.

HERBERT: You'll find this chair here particularly—

RUNCITER: I don't care what my ass is doing; I just care about privacy. Thank you very much, Mister von Vogelsang.

HERBERT: Ella Runciter will be brought in very soon and the electronic hook-up will be in place. Make yourself comfortable; it won't be long.

There follows absolute silence. On the screen ELLA *remains visible with the drops of moisture oozing across the glass above her face; the machinery gauges show occasional changes, and there are "life sign" dots tracing across screens, but she, as an analog to the silence, moves not in the least. The immobility and unchangingness of* ELLA *and the audio silence continue as long as reasonable, stretched out until we feel* RUNCITER's *overwhelming impatience that something happen. Then:*

The machinery connected to ELLA *is abruptly severed by hands reaching down joltingly; she is moved, placed on a dolly; in a swift sequence of efficient actions, like those on the loading dock, like one would expect in a warehouse of stored objects,* ELLA *is transported from where she was, through automatically opening doors, down corridors, past people who are only blurs; the motion is as hectic and bang-bang as the previous episode was static; a cacaphony replaces the silence, too.* ELLA *of course shows no change of expression, but we feel the jolts. This is a warehouse, a morgue, a hospital, this is birth, this is impersonal handling of freight; this yields to:*

6.

RUNCITER *sits in great leather-covered chair, using communications equipment: it is an ancient telephone; it is a ham operator straining to pick up a far-distant weak signal; it is a visitor in jail trying to use the dismal link-up to an inmate; it is even a concerned psychiatrist attempting to catch and discern and comprehend the random mumblings of a near-unconscious patient.* RUNCITER *holds a headphone against one ear and speaks into a PX-operator-*

type bent tube. Straining all the while. Laboring against a faulty connection that sputters in and out and is never, at best, clear or strong enough.

RUNCITER: (*Huskily, with brusque affection*) Hi, Ella.

ELLA: (*Her voice swims groggily, as if recirculating in reverie, outside of time, in oceans that move at such a different rate than* RUNCITER's *mind that although she hears him she cannot adjust.*) Oh . . . hello, Glen.

It is a childlike voice, but most important, its tone shows astonishment; she can't believe that she is hearing from him. For her it is a miracle, and a delightful one. The camera shows her still frozen, still exactly as she was, is, will be, but as it pans up on this we hear her say, in stacatto amazement, as if simultaneously she were sitting up bolt-fast:

ELLA: Glen!!

She is fully alert and conscious, now, demonstrating that the half-lifers are not always in a senile-like state. Her voice is clear; she understands. But it is still a young voice, because for ELLA, *time stopped long ago; she is frozen both in space and in time—outside of each. But this is not a seance; this is no hollow, echoing ghostly voice, as was that of Hamlet's father in "Hamlet."* ELLA's *voice shows her to be at least momentarily real, solid, and here. Communications problems may exist, but* ELLA *is not a departed shade.* RUNCITER *is not speaking to the vitiated dead. She is far away, but she is alive.*

ELLA: How much time has passed?

RUNCITER: Couple years.

ELLA: Tell me what's going on.

RUNCITER: Bunch of bullshit. China developed a vaccine for lymphatic cancer; I know that'd interest you.

ELLA: Yes, wonderful.

RUNCITER: The U.S. banned it. Uh, Ella, everything's going to pieces, the whole organization. That's why I'm here; you wanted to be brought into major policy planning decisions, and god knows we need that now, a new policy, or anyhow a revamping of our scout structure.

ELLA: (*Reflectively*) Glen, I was dreaming. I saw a smoky red light, a horrible light. And yet I kept moving toward it. I couldn't stop.

RUNCITER: Yeah. The *Bardo Thödol*, the Tibetian Book of the Dead, tells about that. You remember reading that; the doctors made you read it when you were—(*Hesitates*) Dying.

ELLA: The smoky red light is bad, isn't it?

RUNCITER: Yeah, you want to avoid it. Listen, Ella. We've got problems. You feel up to hearing about it? I mean, I don't want to overtax you; just say if you're too tired or if there's some other matter you want to hear about or discuss.

ELLA: It's so weird. I think I've been dreaming all this time, since you last talked to me. Is it really two years? Do you know, Glen, what I think? I think that other people around me—we seem to be progressively growing together. A lot of my dreams aren't about me at all. Sometimes I'm a man and sometimes a little boy; sometimes I'm an old fat woman with varicose veins. And I'm in places I've never seen, doing things that make no sense.

RUNCITER: Well, like they say, you're eventually headed for a new womb to be born out of. And that smoky red light—that's a humiliating low sort of womb. You're probably anticipating your next life, or whatever it is. Hey. (*He slaps his knee and tries to smile*) Let me tell you what's happened, what made me come here, and bother you. S. Dole Melipone has dropped out of sight!

There is a moment of silence and then Ella laughs merrily.

ELLA: Who or what is an S. Dole Melipone? There can't be any such thing.

RUNCITER: Maybe you've forgotten.

ELLA: (*Chastened, no longer merry*) He's one of Mr. Hollis' top telepaths. I remember. I'm sorry.

RUNCITER: We've had at least one inertial sticking close to him ever since G.G.Ashwood first scouted him, a year and a half ago. We *never* lose Dole. So I thought, I'll go ask Ella; she'll know what to do. That Hollis with all his telepaths—we know from a bug we put in his bookkeeping office he does a tremendous business in leasing telepaths, and we're the only real threat he has. We're the only . . . (*Pauses, waits*) You can hear me, Ella, right? You're still there?

ELLA: (*Now dreamily*) Step up your ads on TV. Warning business

Philip K. Dick

firms about telepaths invading them. Let the public know the threat and what . . . (*An interval of static on the line; her words are garbled.* RUNCITER *scowls in dismay, holds the headphone against his ear tightly*) Tell me what this Melipone person is like.

RUNCITER: As near as we can tell, Melipone is a money-psi. And with all the inertials it takes to balance his field, he must make—hell, I bet he clears more in a year than I do. Ella? (*Listens, shakes the headphones*)

Hey, hello there, Ella Runciter, wife of Glen Runciter, owner of—(*Again he pauses; the noise of not only static but crosstalk is heard.* RUNCITER's *face is anxious, now*)

Ella, can you hear me? Is something wrong?

RUNCITER *stares at the frozen form of* ELLA *in the nearby casket, his attention turning from it back to the headphones.*

JORY: My name is Jory.

This voice comes from the headphones from which ELLA's *voice has been coming, and although it is a man's, it still contains traces, bizarrely, of the fresh, young, female voice of his wife; it is not so much a different voice, a different person on the line replacing* ELLA, *but her characteristic sounds altered to a rougher pitch, a gross pitch, a rasping and unpleasant pitch, with overtones of metallic savagery.*

RUNCITER: Get off the line! I was talking to my wife Ella; where'd you come from?

RUNCITER *turns from dismay to anger, a powerful anger, that of a strong man.*

JORY: I am Jory and no one talks to me. I'd like to visit with you awhile, mister, if that's okay with you. What's your name?

RUNCITER: I want to talk to Ella Runciter, number 75—my wife, not you.

On RUNCITER's *face a fixed stare appears, as if he senses something more than a mere fouled-up electronic connection, a mere breakdown in the moratorium's communications circuitry.*

JORY: I know Mrs. Runciter. She talks to me, but it isn't the same as somebody like you talking to me, somebody in the world. Mrs. Runciter is here where we are; it doesn't count because she doesn't know any more than the rest of us do. What year is it,

UBIK: The Screenplay

mister? Did they send that android-operated probe to Proxima they were talking about? I wanted to go with that, mister, but I guess it's too late now. You tell me things, mister, and I'll see to it Mrs. Runciter gets told; I'll pass it all on, I'm reliable.

Literally throwing the headphone down, RUNCITER stands, turns toward the office door, does not even move toward it or open it as he bellows:

RUNCITER: Fucking von Vogelsang!!

He stands there, his face distorted and livid, waiting. The office door remains shut, but RUNCITER doesn't budge from where he stands: it is up to HERBERT, the moratorium owner, to come to him. The office door flies open, but:

There is, all at once and without warning, superimposed on the total screen, covering what we've been watching, an Andy Warhol colored-dot type austere graphic representation of a spray can. It is a frozen image that remains. The can is super large, drawn not photographed but drawn in the Warhol absolute fidelity to realism style. There is, however, no writing whatsoever on the spray can, even on its label, which is clearly visible; hence no clue to its contents. No sound, none, accompanies it, and it does not change in any fashion. Since it is drawn and without writing, we understand that despite its fidelity to graphic representationalism, it is incomplete . . . which implies something left out, which implies that there is more—possibly more to come. With no explanation, this phenomenon vanishes and the sequence in progress continues; but it now, at least for a moment, seems somehow in the background, since the can was so large, so gross and blatant, so forward, so between us and the action. So close to us. Something has come between us and what we have been watching, something in a sense more real or anyhow real in a visibly different sense.

HERBERT *enters the office, stammering in response to the summons.*

HERBERT: Is something the matter, Mister Runciter? Can I assist you?

RUNCITER: I've got some *thing* coming in over the wire. Instead of my wife Ella. Damn you guys; what does this mean?

HERBERT: Did the individual identify himself?

RUNCITER: Jory.

HERBERT: Oh yes. That would be, ah, Jory Miller. Believe he's located next to your wife. In the bin.

RUNCITER *turns toward the plastic casket and gazes down at the brown-haired young woman we have been seeing; he shows perplexity, and even fear—it is evident that for him this latter emotion is unusual, or at least it's unusual for him to reveal it; he swiftly covers it up with brusque accusations.*

RUNCITER: But I can see it's Ella!

HERBERT: (*Soothing with efficient professional skill, as he fusses with the communications equipment, as if that's what's at fault, a mere technical difficult easily smoothed over and repaired.*) After prolonged proximity there is, occasionally, a shall I say mutual osmosis, a suffusion between the mentational entities of our half-lifers. Jory Miller's cephalic activity is particularly good; your wife's is not. That makes for an unfortunate one-way passage of interruptive protophasons.

RUNCITER: Can you correct it? (RUNCITER*'s voice is hoarse; he has lost control*) Get this thing out of my wife's mind and get her back—that's your job!

HERBERT: If the technical difficulty persists, your money will be refunded to you.

A moment of silence; RUNCITER *stares at him, not speaking, regaining his self-control, and, too, his mastery of the interpersonal situation. It is evident to us that this verbal magic, fobbed off on him to cover an extraordinarily bad situation, isn't working; he comprehends the gravity of what has happened; after all, Ella is not just another number in the cold-pac bin to him: she is his wife.*

RUNCITER: If you don't get this Jory person off the line, I'll warm up your whole cold-pac area. Our organization has that technical know-how. Every client you have will sue. I won't have to.

HERBERT: Oh really? (HERBERT, *now has lost control; he begins to lose his composure and babble, in the face of* RUNCITER*'s strength and correct appraisal*) Think of two AM radio transmitters, one close by but limited to only five hundred watts of operating power.

RUNCITER: Is she still alive in there?

UBIK: The Screenplay

HERBERT: (*More maturely, more quietly*) When we return her to the bin we won't install her near Jory again. She may—return, once Jory phases out. Plus anyone else who may have gotten into her because of her weakened state. She's accessible to almost anyone. However, if we place her casket—I should say container—in isolation.

While HERBERT *explains,* RUNCITER *walks through the still-open door of the office and down the hall; the camera follows him, so that* HERBERT*'s explanations echo from behind, receding as* RUNCITER *strides along. The babble, muted and meaningless, of other customers blends with* HERBERT*'s voice, plus again the background Beethoven choral music emanating from the corridor wall-speakers.* RUNCITER *halts at a main intersection, evidently confused; he lets people crowd past him and merely stands. No particular expression shows on his face; he is simply a man who might have gotten lost in looking for a particular corridor in the building, and has momentarily paused.*

RUNCITER *reaches into his coat pocket, fishes about slowly, brings forth a pack of Wrigley's spearmint gum; calmly, he draws one stick of gum from it, unwraps it. For a moment he stands studying the writing on the gum-wrapper as, with the other hand, he places the gum in his mouth. He appears to be thinking. Fade out.*

7.

The "conapt" (condominium apartment) of JOE CHIP, *the protagonist of this piece. Chrome and hooked-up appliances can be seen throughout, as if a housewife of the future had made it with the "Dating Game" television show; there are few other possessions in* CHIP*'s conapt, few items which do not plug into the wall outlets and draw electricity. The kitchen in particular is a symposium of power assists, most of them nonessential, all expensive-looking, but with one feature we don't have yet: each has a coin slot with a specific sum (e.g. 25¢ or 10¢) posted. A bus conductor's change-dispenser rests on the left drainboard and several empty cloth coin bags. It's obvious that* CHIP *is an over-extended person in terms of his capabilities.* CHIP *sits at his kitchen table in his bathrobe, inserting coin into a* PAPE *machine: an automated newspaper.*

PAPE: Yes sir. Gossip.

CHIP: Gossip.

PAPE: Guess what Stanton Mick, the reclusive, interplanetarily

Philip K. Dick

known speculator and financier, is up to at this very moment.

The PAPE's *works whizz and a scroll of printed matter creeps from its slot; the ejected roll gets past* CHIP *and bounces onto the floor; he stares down moodily.* CHIP *is a young man, with a dour expression, somewhat bewildered and wry, somewhat equated to his limitations, perhaps too amused by them to overcome them. He reminds us of Jason Robards. Now,* CHIP *retrieves the roll of news, spreads it flat before him. There slowly floats up to fill entire screen the* PAPE's *printout; it hovers before us like some ancient sacred text:*

MICK HITS WORLD BANK FOR TWO TRIL

(AP) London. What could Stanton Mick, the reclusive, interplanetarily known speculator and financier, be up to? the business community asked itself as rumor leaked out of Whitehall that the dashing but peculiar industrial magnate, who once offered to build gratis a fleet by which Israel could colonize and make fertile the otherwise desert areas of Mars, had asked for and may possibly—

CHIP: This isn't gossip. This is speculation about fiscal transactions. I want to know who's sleeping with who and what they're on.

PAPE: Insert ten cents and dial "low gossip."

CHIP, *badgered by the machine into paying twice, searches for and at last locates a coin; puts it in, redials. Another scroll rolls out, and it, too, floats up to occupy the entire screen:*

Accosted by a cutpurse in a fancy N.Y. after-hours stinkpit th'other night, LOLA HERZBERG-BERG bounced a swift right jab off the chops of the do-badder which sent him reeling onto the questionable table of an unidentified miss with astonishingly huge—

Sound of doorbell; the printed matter winks out of existence, and we see CHIP *stumble up, spilling several small objects from his lap. Voice of* G.G. ASHWOOD *from other side of door.*

ASHWOOD: I know it's early, Joe, but I just hit town. G.G. Ashwood, here; I've got a firm prospect I snared in Topeka, I read this one as magnificent and I want your confirmation before I lay the shuck in Runciter's lap. Anyhow, he's in Switzerland.

CHIP: I don't have my test equipment in the apt.

ASHWOOD: Shit, I'll shoot over to the shop and pick it up for you. (ASHWOOD's *voice bubbles with annoying enthusiasm;* CHIP *winces.*) Dearie, this is a sweet number, a walking symposium of miracles that'll curl your pubic hair and the needles of your gauges, and, in addition, give new life to the firm, which it badly needs. And furthermore—

CHIP: It's an anti-what? Anti-telepath?

ASHWOOD: I'll lay it right on you upfront, Joe, I don't know. (ASHWOOD's *voice lowers, now, to confidentiality.*) This is confidential, this one. I can't stand here at the gate gum-flapping away out loud; somebody might overhear. In fact, I'm already picking up the thoughts of some gloonk in a ground-level apt who—

CHIP: Okay! Give me five minutes to get dressed and find out if I've got any coffee around the apt.

ASHWOOD: You'll like her.

CHIP: Pardon? (*Displays panic*) My apt's unfit to be seen; I'm behind in my payments to the building clean-up robots. They haven't wheeled in here in two weeks. (*Pauses, with mixed emotions*) How old is she?

ASHWOOD: How old are you dear? Nineteen.

CHIP: Just a moment. (CHIP *walks away from door to electronic phone on wall; speaks into it very quietly*) Listen. I'm now in a position to divert some of my funds in the direction of settling my bill vis-a-vis your clean-up robots. I'd like them up here right now to go over my apt. I'll pay the full bill, including fines, penalties and interest, when they're finished. (*Silence, as* CHIP *listens to the phone.*)

Okay, I'll charge my overdue bill against my Triangular Magic Key. That will transfer the obligation out of your jurisdiction; on your books it'll show as total restitution. (*Again silence as* CHIP *listens*)

Well, I'll charge that against my Heart-Shaped—what do you mean, I'm on a "basic cash subfloor for the rest of my life?" (CHIP *assumes an inappropriate warm, relaxed tone, now.*)

Philip K. Dick

> You remember that bill in Congress a couple years ago to make the possession of money illegal? My feeling then—

He breaks off. Then hangs up. Stares. Then returns to his kitchen, fishes for change, pays his coffeepot to start up, becomes immersed in this, sniffing the coffee, getting sugar and cream out. At last, carrying cup of coffee, he goes to his conapt door and releases the bolt to open it.

DOOR: Five cents, please.

CHIP, *still holding the cup of coffee, searches his pockets.*

CHIP: I'll pay you tomorrow. (CHIP *tries the knob again, to no avail*) What I pay you is in the nature of a gratuity anyhow. I don't *have* to pay you.

DOOR: I think otherwise. Look into the purchase contract you signed when you bought this conapt. (CHIP *goes from room into other room, finally reappears holding printed form which he's studying, frowningly.*) You discover I'm right.

CHIP, *wordlessly and with no visible emotion, goes to drawer by sink, gets big steel knife, returns to door and begins unscrewing brackets which hold the hasps.*

DOOR: I'll sue.

ASHWOOD: Hey, Joe, baby, it's me! G.G. Ashwood, your fellow employee, remember? Runciter Associates? The rat's ass corporation? And I've got this lady out here—will you open up for me? Open up, Joe. This is business.

CHIP: Put a nickel in the slot for me. The mechanism seems to be jammed on my side.

Sound of coin rattling down; door swings open. Enter ASHWOOD, *salesman type with funny mustache and too-eager body motions and Richard Nixon eyes. With him is one of those girls that as soon as you see her you know you've made a mistake; she is too pretty —black hair, large intense eyes, slender, about 23 years—but her expression is thin and rigid, a mean look, a bitch look, a look of power rather than warmth. It is a clouded face, obscured by an aura of disturbance; there is intelligence here, and the capacity to be kind, but the motor which drives her is one which seeks domination rather than relationship with those around her. This is* PAT CONLEY. *It's as if we are seeing a teenager who has grown in strength and judgment but not in wisdom. Smarter and older than the bubblegummer one sees on the streets,* PAT *is palpably a*

UBIK: The Screenplay

force to be reckoned with; CHIP *gazes at her with that fixed, almost stricken expression which reveals the magnetic tropism which a man of his sort can't dodge. And if* CHIP *can't dodge, he is lost; we see him trapped by the unexpected encounter in his own conapt—snared by the mysterious and the powerful.*

ASHWOOD: This is Pat. Never mind her last name. (ASHWOOD *puts his arm familiarly around* PAT's *waist; she shows no reaction, even aversion.*) Pat, this is the company's highly skilled, first-line electrical type tester.

PAT: Is it you that's electrical? Or your tests?

CHIP: We trade off. (CHIP *glances around at the clutter of his apt uneasily.*) Sit down. Have a cup of actual coffee.

PAT: Such luxury. How can you afford real coffee, Mister Chip?

ASHWOOD: Joe takes in a hell of a lot. The firm couldn't operate without him. (ASHWOOD *reaches for cigarette from pack lying on table.*)

CHIP: Put it back. I'm almost out and I used up my last green ration stamp on the coffee.

ASHWOOD: Listen, Chip. This girl's parents work for Ray Hollis. If they knew she was here they'd give her a frontal lobotomy.

CHIP: They don't know you have a counter talent?

PAT: I didn't understand it myself until your scout sat down with me in the Topeka Kizzutz cafeteria and told me. He said you—

At this moment the scene is blotted out by a repetition of the Andy Warhol type colored-dot graphic representation projected as an opaque superimposition: the spraycan again, in bold lines and hues, but this time writing exists on the previously blank label. We can still hear PAT's *voice; however, it has dimmed to background, as if impeded. The label reads:*

> IF MONEY WORRIES HAVE YOU IN THE CELLAR, GO VISIT THE LADY AT UBIK SAVINGS & LOAN. SHE'LL TAKE THE FRETS OUT OF YOUR DEBTS. SUPPOSE, FOR EXAMPLE, YOU BORROW FIFTY-NINE POSCREDS ON AN INTEREST ONLY LOAN. LET'S SEE, THAT ADDS UP TO (*Words run off label.*)

This holds freeze frame long enough for us to read it all; the type is

Philip K. Dick

bold and clear. PAT *is saying:*

PAT: —could show me objective proof of my anti-talent, with your sophisticated testing hardware.

CHIP: How'd you feel if you did have an anti-talent?

PAT: It seems so—negative. (*Freeze frame of spraycan disappears; scene returns as before*) I can't *do* anything: move objects at a distance or turn stones into bread or give birth without impregnation or reverse the illness process in the sick. Even read minds or look into the future; ordinary psi talents—not even them.

CHIP: But, for the survival of the human race, we need counter-talents to protect us against a race of potential supermen. The anti-psi mutants form a natural restoration of ecological balance. It's nature's way. What is your anti-talent?

PAT: Mister Ashwood explained it to me. I've always had these strange periods in my life, starting in my sixth year. I never told my parents because, you know, I sensed it would displease them.

CHIP: They're precogs?

PAT: Yes.

CHIP: You're right. It would have displeased them. People who can foretell the future get displeased very easily. Especially by anything that comes as a surprise. I'll bet you were a surprise. (CHIP *eyes the girl the way men do: her expression remains impassive.*) But how could you be a surprise to them if they're precogs? You ever tried to surprise a precog, Ashwood?

ASHWOOD: That's not possible, Joe; everybody knows that. Nobody can surprise a precog. Pat can surprise a precog. Do you realize what I'm saying? She goes back in time!

PAT: I don't go back in time. I do something, but Mr. Ashwood has built it up all out of proportion. I think I'll leave.

CHIP: Don't leave.

ASHWOOD: I can read her mind, Joe; she goes back in time. I mean, she can change the past.

CHIP: How do you change the past?

PAT: I think about it. One aspect of it, such as one incident, or something somebody said, a little thing. It only takes a tiny

IF MONEY WORRIES HAVE YOU IN THE CELLAR, GO VISIT THE LADY AT UBIK SAVINGS & LOAN. SHE'LL TAKE THE FRETS OUT OF YOUR DEBTS. SUPPOSE, FOR EXAMPLE, YOU BORROW FIFTY-NINE POSCREDS ON AN INTERST ONLY LOAN. LET'S SEE, THAT ADDS UP TO...

alteration to start a whole different sequence. The first time I did this as a child—

ASHWOOD: When she was six years old, living in Detroit, with her parents of course, she broke this ceramic antique statue. She, Joe, to grow up as a child with precog parents, *two* of them—she *had* to develop this talent.

CHIP: Lamarck's theory of evolution. Acquired characteristics, needed for survival. Otherwise she would have perished. They handed their talent down to her genetically, but she came out altered to suit her own environment; they were the environment. This proves R.A.'s theory, the whole prudence organization is predicated as a segment of society on this theorem: talents such as her parents have generate anti-talents as a survival factor.

PAT: May I take a shower?

CHIP: It costs a quarter.

PAT, *standing up, has begun unbuttoning her blouse;* CHIP *watches fixedly. Gradually he stands, too, facing her.*

PAT: At the kibbutz everything is free.

CHIP: That's impossible. (CHIP *says this as he watches her take off her blouse.*) That's impossible! Are you sure you want to do that? Take off your clothes, I mean?

PAT: You don't remember.

CHIP: (*Hysterically*) Remember? Remember what?

PAT: My not taking off my clothes. In another present. You didn't like that very well, so I eradicated that time-track; hence this, what you see.

CHIP: What did I do, refuse to test you?

PAT: You mumbled something about Mister Ashwood having overrated my anti-talent.

CHIP: I don't work that way; I wouldn't do that.

PAT: Here. (PAT *bends to rummage in the pocket of her discarded blouse; she brings forth a slip of folded paper, which she hands to* CHIP.) From the previous present, the one I abolished.

CHIP *reaches to take the slip; he examines it, then hands it wordlessly back to her.*

ASHWOOD: What did it say?

CHIP: Do not hire.

PAT: Do you need to test me? After seeing that?

CHIP: Well, I have this regular procedure . . .

PAT: You are a little debt-ridden, ineffective bureaucrat who can't even scrounge together enough coins to pay his door to let him into and out of his apartment.

CHIP: (*Offering her coffee*) Sugar? Cream?

PAT: Cream. (*Maintaining his poise,* CHIP *walks to his refrigerator to open it.*)

REFRIGERATOR: Ten cents, please. Five cents for opening, five cents for—

CHIP: It isn't even real cream; it's plain synthetic milk. From plastic cows. Just this one time; I swear I'll pay you back. Tonight.

PAT: (*Tosses him several coins*) Do you want me to bail you out of your problems, Mr. Chip? (*Bare-chested, in her work-jeans and boots, she stands watching him as he tugs futilely at the refrigerator door.*) You know I can. Sit down and write out your evaluation report on me. Forget the tests. My anti-talent is unique anyhow; you can't truly measure the field I generate —it's in the past, and you're testing me in the present, which takes place simply as an automatic consequence.

ASHWOOD: Write the evaluation, Joe. It's best for everyone. And then we can all have a drink.

CHIP: "A drink"? I want breakfast.

ASHWOOD: You want a lot of things, Joe. That you can't have, in life. Maybe this is your chance to get them. This girl is willing to move in with you. She understands your—situation, if you know what I mean. Hell, I'll bet she could even fix breakfast for you, if that's what you want, if that's what you're interested in. You could do that, couldn't you, Pat?

CHIP: Runciter never should have put you on a straight commission basis, Ashwood. Someday you're going to come in here leading a goat. (CHIP, *however, picks up a pad of paper and pen, begins to write; this is what they want and both* PAT *and* ASHWOOD *watch intently.*)

A goat that can raise the dead.

ASHWOOD: (*Pleased*) A goat that can *stop* people from raising the dead.

PAT: When can I move my things in? You know, that money I gave you, Mr. Chip—

CHIP: You want an accounting.

PAT: I will pay half the rent here. And do half the work of keeping things tidy. And buy half the groceries.

CHIP *smiles. It conveys resignation. Nothing more. He tosses them the paper on which he has written.*

8.

The New York offices of Runciter Associates. RUNCITER *striding along corridor. Nothing exceptional in decor, just efficiency and the indices of professionals at work behind many doors. We've caught him in mid-scene; a plump woman wearing heavy glasses, her hair in an old-fashioned bun, is hurrying to keep up with him; this is* ZOE WIRT, *and she is talking.*

WIRT: . . . Mostly, Mr. Runciter, it's telepaths we're having trouble with. Now, my employer considers your organization the foremost: top-rated. He checked into it.

RUNCITER: I know that. Here is how we operate. First we measure the psi field generated so we can tell objectively what we're dealing with. That takes usually from one week to ten days, depending on—

WIRT: My employer wants you to move in your inertials right away. Without the time-consuming and expensive formality of tests.

RUNCITER: We wouldn't know how many inertials to move in, or what kind.

WIRT: My employer is impatient.

RUNCITER: (*He has reached an office door; pauses before entering*) I'll talk to him. Who is he and what's his cable code?

WIRT: You'll deal through me.

RUNCITER: Maybe I won't deal at all. Why won't you tell me who you represent? What is this mumbo-jumbo?

WIRT: There's a security factor in our line of work; my employer traditionally operates this way.

RUNCITER: If telepaths have penetrated your operations, then there is no security factor any longer. Better tell your employer, whoever he is, to face up to that. If we're supplying our personnel, we have to know in advance where they're going to be sent.

WIRT: I can't disclose that, at this time.

RUNCITER: Suppose we never get them back. Strange things happen when you're countering psionic talents. Bad things. Ray Hollis, for example, has been know to kill inertials sent out to negate them. It's my responsibility to see that my people are protected; that's my first duty. The next is to whoever hires us. I can't protect them if I don't know where they are.

RUNCITER *enters the office, in which a number of people sit at futuristic machines, all at work. He approaches an elderly woman whose face is remote and impassive as she sorts through documents; wordlessly, she shows him various documents, but covertly she indicates a lateral print-out scanner on her desk, on which high-speed information passes from left to right:*

MISS WIRT REPRESENTS STANTON MICK. SHE IS HIS CONFIDENTIAL ASSISTANT. THE PROJECT UNDER DISCUSSION EXISTS PRIMARILY ON LUNA. TECHPRISE, MICK'S RESEARCH FACILITIES, IN PROCESS WITH LOW-COST THERMAL SYSTEM & REDUCTION CORE OF NEW ALLOY. LARGE CAPITAL INVESTMENT: HIGH PRIORITY FOR MICK, HENCE SECURITY CONCERN. SPINOFF HOPE: SIDEREAL DRIVE FOR CHEAP COLONIZATION. PREPARED TO FORK-OUT HEAVILY FOR INERTIAL PROTECTION.

RUNCITER: Yes, those are fine, Mrs. Freede.

ELDERLY WOMAN: Thank you, sir. I'll put them through, then.

She continues her ostensibly "routine" work. RUNCITER *turns back to* WIRT, *eyes her.*

RUNCITER: How many inertials do you—does your employer think he wants?

WIRT: He instructed me to opt on the safe side. For security reasons. Forty?

RUNCITER: That's quite a few. *Forty?* I don't have that many uncommitted. I'll give you what I can. Are you sure your employer can afford this? Are you empowered to sign?

WIRT: I'm fully bonded; yes, I can sign and yes, my employer can afford the services of your company.

RUNCITER: We . . . don't usually do business this way. But if time is such a factor for you—(RUNCITER *nods to* ELDERLY WOMAN, *who, without emotional response, already brings forth thick tablet of forms.*) I guess we can skip the prelims and go to the heart of the matter. I'll need your signature in the places where Mrs. Freede has indicated by marking a red X. As to the pro rated amount; I think we can offer you a discount since it would seem—

RUNCITER *breaks off, glancing up as two individuals enter the suite of offices; he stares at them, while* WIRT *obligingly, even smilingly, signs where* ELDERLY WOMAN *indicates on forms. The two people who've entered are* JOE CHIP *and* PAT CONLEY. CHIP *looks disheveled, hung-over, glum.* PAT, *dressed up now, sparkles with allure: she has done more than take a shower, evidently; she wears phosphorescent make-up, and her dress shimmers, and her eyes glow with authority.*

RUNCITER: I gather G. G. Ashwood is back from Topeka.

CHIP: (*In hangdog manner, without enthusiasm*) This is Pat. No last name. (CHIP *hands* RUNCITER *piece of paper, which* RUNCITER *glances at.*)

RUNCITER: She's that good?

RUNCITER *leads the two of them over to the far end of the suite of offices, while* ELDERLY WOMAN *continues to bind* WIRT *contractually;* RUNCITER *now has* PAT *and* CHIP *where* WIRT *can't overhear.*

Listen, I just closed a deal, one hell of a deal. We can use this girl—I was wondering where we'd scare up people; we need everybody who isn't committed. Pull off everyone; this nut dame wants forty inertials—carte blanc, really; look at her, signing away. I haven't even filled in the terms. They must be so scared of infestation . . . anyhow, anyhow —(RUNCITER *now slows down, studies* PAT *for the first time professionally*) What do you counter? What's your anti-talent?

PAT: Anti-ketogenesis.

RUNCITER: What's that?

PAT: The prevention of ketosis. As by the administration of glucose.

CHIP: She's kidding you.

RUNCITER: We're going to Luna. What's "ketosis"? (RUNCITER *stares at* PAT, *baffled.*) I don't understand this girl. She certainly is pretty. Look at those boobs. Joe, you know what? Shit, I flew to Zurich, to that Beloved Brethren Moratorium where Ella is, lying there in cold-pac, you know, this girl reminds me of her; they're both about the same age. Ella's twenty, lying there frozen solid like a haddock, and you know what? You think you got troubles.

CHIP: I didn't say I had troubles.

RUNCITER: Joe, you always have troubles, or what you think are troubles. *I* have troubles, not you. Is this girl shacking up with you there in the shambles? Among the debris and those goddam appliances you owe money to? Anyhow, I'm talking to Ella and this weird freak, this creep from another universe oozes in, some kid named Jory. And he pushes her out of the way! Right out of the way! A fucking parasite. Excuse me, miss. Pat. Sorry. Anyhow, you'll have to excuse me, both of you, because I am distraught. I just got back. Ella's dimming out. (RUNCITER *gets out old-fashioned pocket handkerchief and mops his forehead.*)

We have this deal, see, with this Miss Wirt. It'll pay the overhead for a week. Miss—(RUNCITER *again eyes* PAT *professionally.*)

Will you please go over to personnel where they can fingerprint you to see if you're a chronic child molester or something and we can get going to Luna and set up operations? Joe, I'm renting every inertial I have to this woman—to—listen to this. Stanton Mick. (RUNCITER *still studies* PAT, *but with more gloom, now.*)

You look a lot like Ella but I have the impression, miss, that fundamentally you're quite a different kind of person. How would you like to have a beautiful young wife in cold-pac, miss, and fart around here with these old bags? Sorry. I'm still upset. Joe, it must be terrible there in cold-pac; you're so helpless. You just got to lay there and those parasites devour you. I didn't know about that; I didn't know. We'll all be there someday, you know. In cold-pac. With the real people talking to us. I don't know, maybe it's not worth it.

CHIP: Glen, you'll feel better when we get to Luna and get to work.

RUNCITER: Luna! That's the moon! That's cold, too! Damn near as cold! Colder. It's all colder. The universe is cooling off; I read that somewhere. Entropy, it's called. Equal distribution of heat so it does no useful work. Sounds like you, Joe. Entropy has hit you already. (RUNCITER *slaps* CHIP *on the back with affection.* PAT *regards them coldly, appraisingly, outside their warm friendship.*)

I hope to hell you've tested this girl out thoroughly, Joe, because we need someone good; I hope to hell you haven't screwed the firm up. That's all I need. Well, maybe this Wirt deal will make up for our map-room losing Melipone. Isn't it one of those verities of India that good luck and bad luck come in such a way as to balance each other into celestial harmony? I think I read that somewhere; I forget where. I mean, that's how the universe works.

CHIP: I think it's supposed to all work out for the glory of God.

RUNCITER: Where'd you read that? You know, Joe, it's amazing how much reading goes on in the world. Everybody somewhere is reading something, all the time. Did you ever think of that? Most of what you know you read.

CHIP: Ninety percent.

9.

A further "Andy Warhol" manifestation of a huge spraycan, but this time it swims up slowly, as if rising through water. The words form in patches, joining finally to give us the complete message on the great label. This particular manifestation of the cosmic spraycan does not superimpose over a scene in progress. We hear only the slow lapping of distant ocean waves. The words read:

> WILD NEW UBIK SALAD DRESSING, NOT ITALIAN, NOT FRENCH, BUT AN ENTIRELY NEW AND DIFFERENT TASTE TREAT THAT'S WAKING UP THE WORLD. WAKE UP TO UBIK AND BE WILD! SAFE WHEN TAKEN AS DIRECTED.

Instead of an abrupt, jolting manifestation, this one is leisurely. It

Philip K. Dick

is an interlude. It ages, then, and decays away.

10.

The beaming, smiling, ugly face of ZOE WIRT, *filling the screen.*

WIRT: Welcome to Luna! ! !

ZOE WIRT's *enthusiasm suggests party-time, but now we see the group of* RUNCITER's *inertials, and for them this is serious business; this is a professional assignment. Present are:* JOE CHIP, G.G. ASHWOOD, PAT CONLEY, TIPPY JACKSON *(a thin juiceless girl),* EDIE DORN *(bouncy and energetic but anxious),* FRANCY SPANISH *(sultry and dark, rather squat),* AL HAMMOND *(a balding, wry black dude),* JON ILD *(a small boy),* TITO APOSTOS *(an extremely old man who looks like a Civil War Veteran but with a handlebar mustache),* DON DENNY *(gray-flannel suit company man sort, with horn-rimmed glasses),* SAMMY MUNDO *(terribly fat with deep-set piggish eyes, but a nice smile),* WENDY WRIGHT *(flaxen haired, English beauty, delicate, fair),* FRED ZAFSKY *(looks like a dentist), and of course* RUNCITER *himself who is in charge. The two outstanding-looking women are* PAT *and* WENDY. RUNCITER *is talking to* JOE CHIP.

RUNCITER: It was the Mylax Microdot Corporation. I drove by, and there were these two employees, with flashlights, out in the parking lot, looking all over. On their hands and knees. What I think they did, see, was someone was taking inventory, and it being a microdot corporation, their entire inventory was probably no larger than—

CHIP: Their entire inventory stuck to someone's shoe.

RUNCITER: Now, this is what I mean about information. You can shrink anything down—circuitry, for example. Super-miniaturize it until it's literally at submolecular level. You theoretically could stick all the knowledge of the entire human race into one microdot and then lose it out in the parking lot. Can you imagine how you'd feel?

CHIP: Boss, I lost the entire library at Alexandria. It's out back somewhere near where I parked my car.

RUNCITER: You drank it with your Coke. The knowledge of thirty centuries. The alphabet. How to build a wheel. What is fire. The Congressional Record. The Bible. Listen, Joe. I don't like this. We're not on home ground.

UBIK: The Screenplay

Both RUNCITER *and* CHIP *glance uneasily about at the dome-like structure their group is within.*

RUNCITER: I sense something.

CHIP: Stanton Mick is a reputable financier—I was hearing about him on the news the other day.

RUNCITER: There are wheels within the wheels of reality, Joe. Nothing is the way it looks. Nothing. Joe, our whole group is here. Fourteen of us, including me. You know what Ray Hollis and his freaks would do if they knew we were in one basket, so to speak, like this? A bunch of eggs waiting to be—whatever the expression is. I really do not like this.

Now we see CHIP *take some initiative. He walks over to* PAT; *standing by her he speaks in a low voice.*

CHIP: I hired you; prove you can do something.

PAT: I can do something.

CHIP: I mean besides swivel your crotch.

This was a mistake, this snide, apprehensive remark. PAT'*s head jerks; she stares at him; her face shows many bad, hateful scenes taking place inside her head. Pan up onto her glowing black eyes.*

11.

There manifests itself directly before JOE CHIP, *literally breaking through the dome-structure around him, a stately, gentle scene: a rare coin shop on Fifth Avenue in New York. It comes without sound, visible but silent. Passers-by are visible; it is a moving scene, alive, entering his reality and taking it over so that he is there—he is, in fact, gazing with some interest at the display of coins in the window.*

CHIP:(*Meditating inwardly to himself*) I can't afford it. A three-dollar gold piece—they probably don't even have one. But still, it wouldn't hurt to look. (CHIP *moves closer to study the display of rare coins*) It certainly would make my collection worth a lot more—as an investment—I mean, it would be practical.

TIPPY JACKSON: Mister Chip?

CHIP: (*Still ruminating inwardly*) *What* collection? I don't collect coins. What the hell am I doing here? How the hell long have

Philip K. Dick

I—

TIPPY JACKSON: Mister Chip, I'd very much like to talk to you a moment, if I may. I've been wanting to since we came here. Mister Chip, I've been having some awfully strange experiences and I thought maybe, you know, you could shed some light on them? If I could have a minute of your time? Mister Chip, does it mean anything if you dream poetry, whole lines of it, like whole *pages*, that you don't know? That you have no way of knowing? I mean, how would you know it to dream it? I finally found it in a book. I looked it up.

CHIP: (CHIP *now can see her; he turns his head, bewildered; his experience has disoriented him.*) Where's Pat?

The Lunar dome is back; the group of Runciter Associates inertials can be seen again as before; the rare coin shop and sidewalk traffic are gone; all is as it was; evidently this was some kind of mere head-trip by CHIP. *But:*

TIPPY JACKSON: Oh, yes, your wife.

CHIP: What?

TIPPY JACKSON: More domestic quarreling, I guess. You two are always at it, aren't you. I remember when you both first came to the firm; I personally thought you were perfectly matched. But I guess sometimes one person grows but the other . . .

CHIP: "My wife."

TIPPY JACKSON: Can I tell you about my strange dream? It was just before Mister Runciter telephoned me to say we were to get packed to come here to Luna; in fact his phone call woke me up.

CHIP: My *wife?*

TIPPY JACKSON: Yes, that old bag. Well, she has aged since you first got married. I—didn't mean that. Can I tell you about my dream?

CHIP: Sure.

TIPPY JACKSON: In my dream someone is talking to me. Very insistently. A man's voice, very ugly. Blech. Over and over again, attracting my attention, you know? (TIPPY *mimics hoarse, coarse male voice.*) "I'll bet you talk to my brother Bill. Here, Bill; talk to this lady. Do you like this lady?" (TIPPY *assumes her normal voice again.*) And then I see them, both of them. Bill and Matt. Brothers. Great pale teeth, like trolls have. Yeeg!! Teeth like shovels. And then Bill starts reciting poetry. (TIPPY *again mimics hoarse male voice.*) " 'I, that am curtailed of this fair proportion, cheated of feature by dissembling nature, deformed, unfinished, sent—' " (TIPPY *speaks normally again.*) I forget the rest. It's from Shakespeare's *Richard the Third.* They were talking about themselves. Bill and Matt. That's how they looked, like Richard the Third.

CHIP: Nobody knows how Richard the Third looked.

TIPPY JACKSON: I do. And then I said, "What does that mean," and they said, listen to this, Mister Chip; they said, "It means that we're going to get you."

Silently, JOE CHIP *walks away from her, back to* RUNCITER; *halting, he sees that* PAT *is with* RUNCITER; *they are talking.*

RUNCITER: Joe, you two should kiss and make up. You're going to screw up this whole operation otherwise. As I was saying to Mrs. Chip just now, I'm all for assembling everyone and heading back to Earth, and the hell with this here; it stinks, Joe. Doesn't it, Mrs. Chip? Don't you sense it? See, Joe, your wife senses it, and her judgment has always been good, almost as good as mine. What do you say, Joe? Do you agree?

CHIP: (*Gently, to* PAT) I'm sorry, honey. For yelling at you.

He puts his arms around her, embraces her; sees, then, as camera moves in, the wedding ring on her finger.

PAT: It's okay. We're all tense. Glen's right; there is something peculiar about this assignment; it's not like the others, and yet I can't say why either.

FRANCY SPANISH: Mister Runciter—you, too, Mister Chip, while I have you both together. Two nights ago I received a particularly impressive visitation.

CHIP *and* RUNCITER *together turn and eye her.*

RUNCITER: So? (*Nudges* CHIP)

FRANCY SPANISH: A throng of precogs and telepaths descended from a ladder spun of finest natural hemp to the balcony outside my window. They dissolved a passageway through the wall and manifested themselves around my bed, waking me up with their chatter. They quoted poetry and languid prose

Philip K. Dick

> from oldtime books, which delighted me; they seemed so—sparkling. One of them, who called himself Bill—

Other inertials have clustered about them, now.

TITO APOSTOS: Wait a minute. I had a dream like that, too.

TIPPY JACKSON: Mister Chip, I was just telling you my own dream . . .

RUNCITER: Joe, you should have said something to me. These aren't dreams.

FRANCY SPANISH: Of course not. They're visitations. I can distinguish the difference.

DON DENNY: Sure you can, Francy. (*Winks at* CHIP)

JON ILD: I had a dream but it was about hovercars. I was memorizing the license plate-numbers. I memorized sixty-five, and I still remember them. Want to hear them?

STANTON MICK *appears, the man who has hired them. Elevator doors slide back; everyone turns to look. Potbellied, thick-legged, swarthy, like a great bearded baby, he perambulates toward* RUNCITER *and* CHIP. MICK *is an old pirate, a self-made monster, with no class but lots of pull. He is the industrial spider of their society, who can buy what he wants and whom he wants.*

MICK: Hello, all you top anti-psis! The exterminators are here—by that I mean yourselves. (MICK's *voice has an oddly squeaking, penetrating quality, metallic, like a swarm of bees; it startles everyone: they fall silent.*) The plague, in the form of assorted psionic riffraff, descended upon the harmless, friendly, peaceful world of Stanton Mick. What a day that was for us in Mickville—as we call our attractive and appetizing Lunar settlement here. You have, of course, already started work, as I knew you would. (CHIP *and* RUNCITER *exchange uneasy glances.*) That's because you're *tops* in your field, as everyone realizes when Runciter Associates is mentioned. I'm already delighted at your activity, with the one small exception that I perceive your field-tester there dingling with his, ahem, equipment. Tester, would you look my way while I'm addressing you?

CHIP: Yes sir.

CHIP *shuts off the nearby power-unit; the gauges of his nearby equipment, and the moving "life signs" dots cease to register.*

UBIK: The Screenplay

RUNCITER: Leave your equipment on. You're not an employee of Mister Mick. You're my employee.

WENDY: (WENDY *takes hold of* CHIP*'s arm, presses nervously against him.*) He certainly is an odd one, Joe. He gives me the shivers.

All the inertials, now, are clustering together, as if for mutual protection. PAT *glances frigidly at* WENDY *holding onto* JOE CHIP *but doesn't speak; her look, however, shoots daggers.*

CHIP: It doesn't matter anyhow.

RUNCITER: What do you mean? How great is the psi field here?

CHIP: There is no field.

RUNCITER: You mean we're nullifying it?

CHIP: I mean there are no telepaths, no precogs, no nothing within range of my equipment. Except our own counter-field. We're countering nothing. There is nothing. Just us.

RUNCITER: That's fucked!

CHIP: I know that's fucked. What'd we come here for? Why'd they hire us?

DON DENNY: Maybe they're just paranoid about having been infiltrated.

RUNCITER: (RUNCITER *walks slowly toward* STANTON MICK.) Mister Mick, where did you get the idea that Psis had infiltrated your operations here on Luna? And why didn't you allow us to run our tests initially? Did you know we'd get this result, which is no result? Do you mind explaining? (*Abruptly* RUNCITER *turns back toward* CHIP *and the others, speaking briskly, rapidly to them, giving them sharp commands.*) Let's get the hell back to Earth; let's get out of here. (RUNCITER *raises his voice.*) Collect your possessions; we're flying back to New York. I want all of you in the ship within fifteen minutes; if you can't get your shit together by then, forget your shit. (STANTON MICK *stands there grinning inanely as* RUNCITER *orders his inertials into quick action.*) Joe, leave your equipment; forget your equipment! (RUNCITER*'s face shows alarm.*) Why's Mick grinning like that? He's a freak! They're freaks here!

STANTON MICK, *still speaking in his metallic insect-like voice, floats up to the ceiling of the dome, his arms protruding distendedly*

53

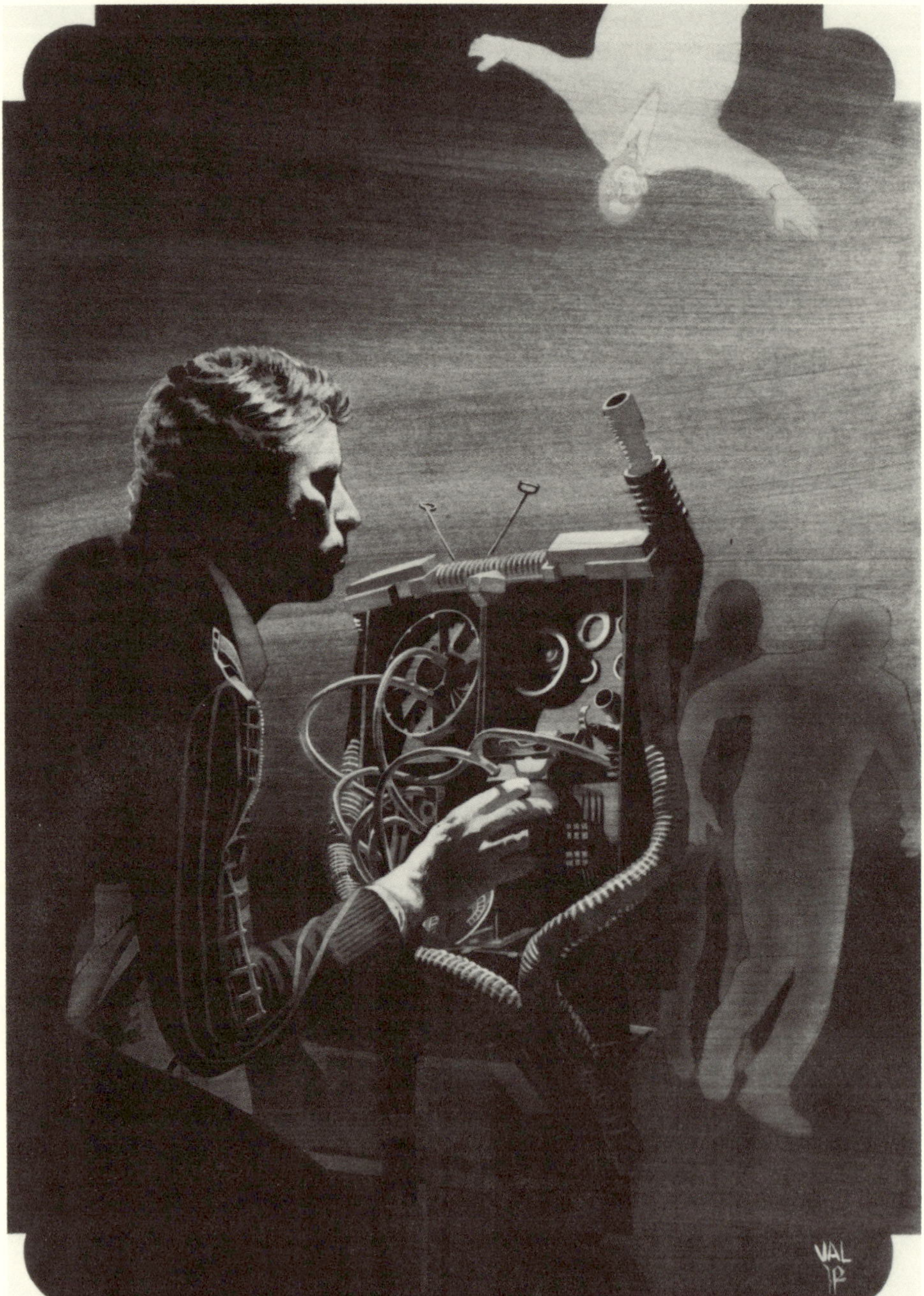

UBIK: The Screenplay

and rigidly. He—it—resembles a balloon. The sight is macabre, both funny and terrifying together.

MICK: Mister Runciter, don't let your thalamus override your cerebral cortex. This matter calls for discretion, not haste. Calm your people down and let's huddle together in a mutual effort to bring about understanding.

MICK's colorful, rotund body bobs about, twisting in a slow, gradual, transversal rotation so that now his feet, rather than his head, are extended in RUNCITER's *direction. Finally* MICK *is entirely upsidedown, his feet against the dome ceiling, his head facing the floor. The absurd, comical, mechanical quality reveals that this is not—cannot be—a human being. Every person in the dome runs away en masse, in instinctive panic.*

RUNCITER: It's a self-destruct humanoid bomb! Help me get everybody out of this place! They just now put it on auto; that's why it floated upward—it got out of control.

The bomb which had posed as STANTON MICK *detonates. Special effects concussion and chaos, but out of it emerges what appears to be some kind of peculiar tablet or sign, anyhow a square on which writing is inscribed, as follows:*

IT TAKES MORE THAN A BAG TO SEAL IN FOOD FLAVOR. IT TAKES UBIK PLASTIC WRAP—ACTUALLY FOUR LAYERS IN ONE. KEEPS FRESHNESS IN, AIR AND MOISTURE OUT. WATCH THIS SIMULATED TEST.

Around the square of vivid writing materializes the spraycan 'a la Andy Warhol; the square of writing becomes its label, as in previous manifestations. The chaos and tremors of the explosion, however, are not reduced to "Batman" animated drawings; they remain actual, and only the spraycan is painted rather than photographed. Swirls of dust, the debris of the dome, obscure the spraycan and its writing, like the mists of deep space or time, giving it a solemn, mysterious quality. And then without warning the drawing of the spraycan and the writing burst apart like a paper sign; they are destroyed by fire, blasted by explosion; all is ruin, all comes at us at enormous velocity. The two realities —the spraycan versus the actual photographed events—merge into one ruin of particles, as if an entire planet had burst, and nothing remains of it but radioactive waste. It is as if the Warhol drawing of the spraycan and writing attempted somehow to stem the

Philip K. Dick

explosion and did so—but only for a moment; then it, too, was swept away. Even it was not enough.

12.

The Lunar dome, deformed and brutalized by the explosion; it is transformed into a spectacle of misery. Ghostly pale shapes grope about blindly, making feeble and inappropriate motions; the air is thick with dust in suspension. But most of all, flying rubble has punctured the dome; servo-assist mechanisms, automatic in nature, have hurried to seal against the loss of air into the Lunar void, and the rushing in of the deathly cold. Frost, like the stark power of winter, death-dealing and terrible, lies over everything in a uniform coating: over the moving forms, the wreck of CHIP's *equipment, walls, ceiling and floors. The moving shapes shiver as they stumble. Dimly, in the background, we see red-lit illuminated signs: SUB THERMAL DROP! SUB THERMAL DROP! The whine of emergency equipment can be heard. Although the humans are bewildered, the robot mechanisms are not. Looming up,* JOE CHIP *stands hunched over, coughing.*

DON DENNY: (*Excitedly*) They killed Runciter, Mister Chip. That's Mister Runciter.

AL HAMMOND: They forgot to shut off their servo-assists, Mister Chip. I think that's what saved us. Oversight.

CHIP: Well, you know, that's the sort of thing, those are what does it. Makes the difference. They rig up that humanoid bomb that walks and talks and then they leave all the mechanisms on and they jump in and repair every goddam leak in the dome the explosion made right away.

CHIP *bends down awkwardly over the inert body of* RUNCITER.

ASHWOOD: Joe, shit, man, we got to get the hell out of here! Come on, man! (*Tugs at* CHIP *urgently*)

FRANCY SPANISH: Joe, you're in charge.

CHIP: Yeah. (CHIP *straightens up, stands.*) Who else is dead?

WENDY *appears from the swirling dust to stand close by him, again intimately taking his arm, as if by habit.*

WENDY: I — think everyone else is hurt but alive.

CHIP: They must have left the mechanisms on because their own personnel are still in the dome. Too risky to . . .

UBIK: The Screenplay

AL HAMMOND: (*Quietly*) Joe, get us out of here. Now. Or we'll be dead, too.

CHIP: Okay, how many of you have hand weapons?

AL HAMMOND: You fire a handgun you will pierce the dome wall.

CHIP: Well, I want to kill a couple of them.

EDIE DORN: You are responsible for the lives of twelve people. Mister Runciter wanted to leave; I heard him say so; that's what we should do now.

ILD: (*Stammering*) We c-c-c-can come back later, Mister Chip, and kill them. Okay? Can we d-d-d-do it later instead?

CHIP: (*Now* CHIP *has begun to take command; his confusion is diminishing.*) Main thing is, we should get Glen Runciter into cold-pac.

AL HAMMOND: There's cold-pac facilities in the ship. His own —standby. For the day.

There now follows a series of scenes in which their slain leader is carried, in the fashion that the slain Siegfried was returned to his kin upon shields, from the dome.

13.

Outside of dome, on Lunar surface; the causeway connecting the dome with Runciter Associates' parked ship, Pratfall Two. *No one speaks; they just carry, lugging a few possessions as well as* RUNCITER, *especially the women. No sign of the adversary. Boarding the ship; servo-mechanisms shoot out to receive them on signal from them.*

14.

Inside ship; hurriedly they all convey RUNCITER *to the small cold-pac storage locker, which, unlike what we saw at the moratorium, is upright. Much effort, sweating, wasted motion, but they get it done. From their labors it's obvious that it was easy to get to Luna, difficult to get back to Earth. A warning signal indicates imminent take-off; the propulsion system screams ear-splittingly; each person seizes emergency hold-bars — not seat-belt type set straps — and the ship is airborne, strewing everything not nailed down in random showers around them. It's obvious they're leaving as rapidly as possible. Dissolve.*

Philip K. Dick

Later, same scene; calm, at least of a mechanical sort, has returned; the flight is smooth and level. Each person is seated, now, since there is no present thrust. They hold on less than our average bus passenger.

PAT: Anyone have a cigarette?

CHIP: (CHIP *sits by her hunched over, melancholy and brooding.*) Cigarette. (CHIP *searches reflexively in his pockets, brings out a pack.*) His brain may have deteriorated. Too much time.

DON DENNY: There's no communication circuit to the cold-pac here in the ship?

CHIP: We'll have to wait. Christ, we may have to move R.A.'s offices to the Beloved Brethren Moratorium in Zurich, now. They're both going to be there.

AL HAMMOND: Yeah, if we're lucky.

CHIP *is staring at the cigarettes; he crumples one, and fragments of dried fibers scatter like chaff; he continues to stare.*

CHIP: Am I really married to you?

PAT: Why do you ask that?

CHIP: These cigarettes . . . they're dried out. Like they're a thousand years old.

PAT: What's the connection between that and our marriage?

AL HAMMOND: The bomb blast. The heat.

CHIP: You know, something like this ages you. I'm worn out; there's nothing left of me.

WENDY: I can't wait to get back to Earth. It's Ray Hollis, isn't it? We never were in touch with Stanton Mick.

CHIP: Not unless Stanton Mick is a balloon. A helium-filled metal balloon primed with C-twelve.

FRANCY SPANISH: Is helium lighter than nothing? Because there is no air on the moon. Just nothing.

AL HAMMOND: Worse than nothing. They were waiting for us.

"Andy Warhol" manifestation superimposed of the spraycan; its label this time reads:

PERK UP POUTING HOUSEHOLD SURFACES WITH

UBIK: The Screenplay

NEW MIRACLE UBIK, THE EASY-TO-APPLY, EXTRA-SHINY, NONSTICK PLASTIC COATING. ENTIRELY HARMLESS IF USED AS DIRECTED. SAVES ENDLESS SCRUBBING, GLIDES YOU RIGHT OUT OF THE KITCHEN!

CHIP: Give me the ship's phonebook. I'll call the moratorium.

TIPPY JACKSON *brings him phonebook.* CHIP *leafs through it; the phonebook is modernesque, with a magnifying lens and high-speed sorting system.* CHIP *types out onto small request box of phonebook, waits.*

PHONEBOOK: This is a recording. The number which you have given me is obsolete. If you need assistance, place a red card in—

CHIP: What's the date on this thing? (CHIP *examines phonebook, scowling.*) 1990. Two years old.

EDDIE DORN: That can't be. This ship didn't exist two years ago. Everything on it is new.

TITO APOSTOS: Maybe Runciter cut a few corners.

ASHWOOD: Glen Runciter lavished care, money and engineering skill on *Pratfall Two*. Everybody who ever worked for him knows that; this ship is —was— his pride and joy.

CHIP: (*Inserting red card into phonebook*) Give me the Beloved Brethren Moratorium in Zurich, Switzerland. Phonocode 30-20 or something. This is an emergency.

Viewscreen of phone lights up; HERBERT's *face appears.*

HERBERT: I am Herr Herbert Schoenheit von Vogelsang. Have you come to me in your grief, sir? May I take your name and address, were it to take place that we got cut off?

CHIP: There's been an accident.

HERBERT: What we deem an "accident" is ever yet a display of God's handiwork. In a sense, all life could be called an "accident." And yet, when we peer more closely—

CHIP: I don't want to get into a theological discussion, not at this time!

HERBERT: This is the time, out of all times, when the consolations of theology are most soothing. Is the deceased a relative?

CHIP: Yeah, our employer, Glen Runciter of Runciter Associates, New York. You have his wife Ella there. We'll be landing in eight minutes. Have one of your crews ready at the Zurich field.

HERBERT: Is he in cold-pac now?

CHIP: No! He is warming himself on the beach at Tampa, Florida, grabbing every ass that passes by.

HERBERT: I'm afraid the hot sun—

CHIP: Have your crew and a transport van at the airfield and stand by. (CHIP *hangs up; glares morosely.*) I'm going to phone Ray Hollis and kill him. For bringing this about. If God had approved of half-life, we'd have been born in a baggy of dry ice. Like a lid of frozen grass. And spent our time here thawing out.

DON DENNY: (*At the controls of the ship*) We're now under the jurisdiction of the Zurich micro-wave transmitter. It'll bring us in; we can relax.

EDIE DORN: You know, Joe, it could have been a lot worse; we all could be dead.

CHIP: I always was suspicious of a place that doesn't have air. Why would they build a place without air? I wonder sometimes about the great cosmic planner; no air, no water, just rocks and lots of room to die.

AL HAMMOND: Joe, you're going to have to break the news to Ella.

CHIP: They can break the news to each other. Let the half-dead talk to the half-dead.

WENDY: Not half-dead. Half-*alive*. (WENDY *scrutinizes* CHIP *with affection.*) It's you who look half dead.

15.

The Zurich airfield. Pratfall Two *parked on its tail; hovertruck marked* BELOVED BRETHREN MORATORIUM *linked to it and transfer of Runciter's cold-pac unit taking place by moratorium technicians. The Runciter Associates inertials are meandering toward the field's installations, specifically the coffee shop.* CHIP *starts to push open coffee shop door.*

COFFEE SHOP DOOR: Five cents, please.

CHIP *waits until a couple exeunts from the coffee shop; they hold the door and he goes inside.*

16.

Interior of coffee shop. Computer run; no personnel.

CHIP: Coffee.

RULING MONAD CIRCUIT: Cream or sugar? (*Clicks in response to his nod*) Yessir. (*Tiny doors fly open; space-program-like containers appear.*) One international poscred, please.

CHIP: Charge this to the account of Glen Runciter of Runciter Associates, New York.

RULING MONAD CIRCUIT: Insert the proper credit card, please.

CHIP: They haven't let me carry a credit card in five years. I'm still paying off what I charged back in—

RULING MONAD CIRCUIT: One poscred, please. (*Audible whine*) Or in ten seconds I will notify the police. The German police. (CHIP *hands a poscred—paper money—over.*) We can do without your kind.

CHIP: (*Fury, pent-up till now, bursts out of him.*) One of these days people like me will rise up and overthrow you, and the end of tyranny by the homeostatic machine will have arrived. The day of human values and compassion and simple warmth will return, and when that happens someone like myself who has gone through an ordeal and who genuinely needs hot coffee to pick him up and keep him functioning when he has to function will get the hot coffee whether he happens to have a poscred readily available or not. (CHIP *lifts miniature pitcher of cream, then sets it down.*)

And furthermore, your cream or milk or whatever it is, is sour. (*Silence from the* RULING MONAD CIRCUIT *of the coffee shop.*)

Aren't you going to do anything? You had plenty to say when you wanted a poscred.

Door of coffee shop opens; AL HAMMOND *enters, seats himself beside* CHIP.

AL HAMMOND: The moratorium jokers have Runciter in their truck. They're ready to take off and they want to know if you intend to ride with them.

CHIP: Look at this cream. This is what you get for one poscred in one of the most modern, technologically advanced cities on

Philip K. Dick

> Earth. I'm not leaving here, Al, until this place makes an adjustment, either returning my poscred or giving me a replacement pitcher of fresh cream so I can drink my coffee.

AL HAMMOND: What's the matter, Joe?

CHIP: First my cigarette. Then the two-year-old obsolete phonebook in the ship. And now they're serving me week-old clotted up sour cream with purple mold growing on it. I don't get it, Al.

As he talks, CHIP *is picking up the coffee cup and staring at the coffee itself, his face showing perplexity. And growing dismay.*

AL HAMMOND: Come on, Joe; forget the coffee—it isn't important. What matters is getting Runciter to the moratorium and finding out if he's—

CHIP: You know who gave me the poscred? Pat Conley. And right away I did what I always do with money; I frittered it away on nothing. On last year's cup of coffee—this coffee is stone cold, Al, totally stone cold. How about coming with me to the moratorium? I need back-up help, especially when I go to confer with Ella. What should we do, blame it on Runciter? He took us there; it's the truth.

AL HAMMOND: (*Rising*) Well, let's get going.

17.

Lounge of Beloved Brethren Moratorium. AL HAMMOND *and* JOE CHIP *sit waiting together.*

AL HAMMOND: Cigarette?

CHIP: All the cigarettes in the world are stale.

AL HAMMOND: Yeah, you're right. (*Throws pack away*)

CHIP: If Runciter were alive, sitting out here in this lounge, everything would be okay. I'm going to miss him.

AL HAMMOND: We may have gotten him into cold-pac soon enough.

CHIP: I'm going to phone Ray Hollis' organization.

AL HAMMOND: Let the police take care of—

CHIP: No, I want to talk to one of their precogs. Find out if this Vogelsang creature can revive Runciter.

UBIK: The Screenplay

CHIP *borrows coin from* HAMMOND, *goes to pay videophone.*

PAY PHONE: I am sorry, sir, but I can't accept obsolete money.

Coin clatters out of return slot.

CHIP: What do you mean? Since when is a North American Freedom Confederation quarter obsolete money?

PAY PHONE: I am sorry, sir, but the coin you put in me was a recalled issue of the United States Philadelphia mint. It is merely of numismatical interest now.

CHIP *examines the coin; for that moment a montage of the moratorium and scene eleven, the New York Fifth Avenue rare coin shop and passers-by, swirls around him; then the moratorium scene takes over again.*

CHIP: George Washington.

CHIP *lifts head; again scene eleven, the coin shop;* CHIP *holding the rare old U.S. silver quarter, starts toward its entrance; we sense something ominous if he goes farther, but he halts, puzzled; the coin shop again is gone, this time totally.*

CHIP: I wonder what it's worth.

MORATORIUM EMPLOYEE: Having difficulties, sir? I saw the phone expel your coin.

EMPLOYEE *provides slug for phone and departs.*

CHIP: I could have made a fortune. They would have bought this coin.

CHIP, *preoccupied, dials phone.*

HOLLIS RECEPTIONIST: Hollis Talents. Oh, Mister Chip. Mister Hollis left word that you'd be calling. We've been expecting you all afternoon. Just a moment, please; I'll put you through. (*Interval. We hear music from the hall speakers: the "Verdi Requiem." It was already there, but unnoticed.*) Go ahead, Mister Chip.

On viewscreen of phone appears a toad-like bloated face, grimacing in mockery at CHIP; *this is* RAY HOLLIS, *their adversary.*

CHIP: Mister Hollis . . .

HOLLIS: Yes, Mister Chip.

CHIP: Mister Hollis . . . as long as I have you on the phone—

Philip K. Dick

But now HERBERT, *the moratorium owner, approaches* CHIP, *an expression of tragic commiseration on his face. It is obvious that the news is bad; what they feared most.* CHIP, *seeing this, hangs the receiver up.*

HERBERT: We did what we could. The signal from him should have bounced out clear and strong, but all we got from the amplification stages was a sixty cycle hum. Just a hum. I'm sorry. I'm very sorry.

CHIP: I'll tell Ella. I'll talk to her.

AL HAMMOND: (*Approaching*) Not now. Tell her tomorrow. Go home and get some sleep.

CHIP: To *Pat Conley*? I can't cope with her either. She's worse than somebody being dead, my friend being dead.

HERBERT: You must bear in mind that we here did not supervise the original cold-pac installation. It was out of our hands.

CHIP: I remember. I'm remembering now.

AL HAMMOND: Take a hotel room here in Zurich, then.

CHIP: You know what I feel like? Doing, I mean. Wendy Wright. Well, that's badly put.

AL HAMMOND: I know what you mean; I know how you feel about her. I'll get her over there.

CHIP: I can get her over there; I just can't get the goddam hotel room. I can talk to people; Wendy especially, but not objects. I'm tired of trying to reason with objects. Like, what'll I pay the hotel room with? It won't take my money any more than the phone did. You didn't see what the phone did with the coin I put into it. You'd have thought I paid it with a dog turd. Everything is screwed; I'm paying one unreasonable object with another unreasonable object and they don't fit. You suppose where Glen Runciter is, there's things yammering at him, too? You suppose he's somewhere trying to fit Part A into Slot B and it won't go because the whole fucking kit is made up of parts left over from six other kits? I give up. I really do; I finally give up. You know, what gets me—what really gets me—is, Ray Hollis was expecting my call. (CHIP *searches his pockets.*) I'm going to phone him back.

AL HAMMOND: Here's some money. (*Sorts among the bills in his wallet*) These are in circulation, old but still in circulation.

UBIK: The Screenplay

These aren't. (*Gives the good ones to CHIP*) There's enough there for the hotel room for one night, dinner and a couple of drinks for both of you. I'll send a R.A. ship from New York tomorrow to pick you and her up.

CHIP: I'll pay you back. I'll be drawing a higher salary now; I'll be able to pay all my debts off, including the back taxes, penalties and fines which the government income-tax people—

AL HAMMOND: Without Pat Conley or with her?

CHIP: I can throw her out now.

AL HAMMOND: I wonder.

CHIP: This is a new start for me, a new lease on life.

AL HAMMOND: In my opinion you have a will to fail. You'll find a way.

CHIP: No, what I actually have is a will to succeed. Glen Runciter saw that; that's why he set up the by-laws so upon his death I'd take over Runciter Associates. What hotel do you recommend?

18.

Zurich hotel room, the transient elegance of the chrome-plated and plastic. JOE CHIP *sprawled out on kingsize bed, in his colorful drawers. He stares in amazement, then rises to his feet unsteadily, goes to phone, dials single digit for room service.*

RUNCITER: (*Voice from phone*) . . . pay him back if at all possible. First, of course, it has to be established whether Stanton Mick actually involved himself, or if a mere homosimulacric substitute was in action against us, and if so why, and if not then how they happened to bring no back-up operation to bear, if any of us survived the blast. It would appear that Mick generally acts in a reputable manner and in accord with legal and ethical practices established throughout the system. In view of this . . . (CHIP *hangs up phone, stands staring dizzily, confounded by what—and whom—he has heard. Again he picks up the receiver.*) . . . lawsuit by Mick, who can afford and is accustomed to litigation of this kind. Our own legal staff certainly should be consulted before we make a formal report to the Prudence Society. It would be libel if made public and grounds for a suit claiming defamation of . . .

CHIP: *Runciter!*

Philip K. Dick

RUNCITER: ... unable to verify probably for at least ...

CHIP *hangs up. Goes into the bathroom, splashes water on his face, combs his hair, goes to toilet, shaves with one-time-use hotel shaver, uses dispenser of aftershave, all done very methodically. At last he emerges, slapping talc on his neck and face, and studying the phone. He goes to the phone again; getting his wallet out he carefully looks up a number, then dials.*

RUNCITER: (*Voice from phone*) ... not the ideal person to manage the firm, in view of his confused personal difficulties, particularly ...

CHIP: Shit.

CHIP *hangs up angrily, goes to chair, sits. Time passes. Then he rises once more, goes over to coin-operated futuristic electronic construct in corner; puts coin in.*

PAPE: Hi! I'm your homeopape machine, a high-speed special service supplied exclusively to all of the fine Schreiber hotels throughout Earth and the colonies. Simply dial the classification of information you wish, and in a matter of seconds I'll swiftly and accurately provide you with a fresh, up-to-the-minute printout tailored to your individual requirements!

CHIP: Okay. I can use some information.

PAPE: You must dial, sir. I can't hear you; I can see your lips moving but I have no audio inputs. (CHIP *examines the dial, then dials it.*) Personal heartaches, yes sir.

As with our Xerox machines, printed sheet slides out; CHIP *takes hold of it and scrutinizes it. Then, abruptly, he wheels and strides across hotel room to closet door; he tugs door open. Pan up. There, within, on the floor of the closet, lies a huddled heap, dehydrated, almost mummified. Decaying shreds like cloth—bending, he turns it gingerly over, his face registering acute horror. Now, hands trembling, he picks it up; it is very light in weight, and he unfolds it—it rustles like dried paper as it unfolds thin bony extensions. Wiry and tangled, the cloud of flaxen hair obscures WENDY's face.*

CHIP: My god, it's *old*. Completely dried-out. Centuries ... like baked in a kiln.

CHIP *drops it with aversion.*

19.

UBIK: The Screenplay

The New York offices of Runciter Associates. The group of inertials sit about, with AL HAMMOND *as their temporary leader; he sits hunched over broodingly, writing on a tablet of paper.* WAYLES, *a fussy little bureaucrat of the organization, is berating* AL HAMMOND.

WAYLES: You people should not have left Mister Chip in Zurich. We can do nothing legally until he arrives here.

AL HAMMOND: I sent the ship; he should be here any time now.

PAT: He probably couldn't get the ship started. Lost the ignition key.

AL HAMMOND: He'll be here.

AL HAMMOND *studies his list.*

DON DENNY: What've you got written there?

AL HAMMOND: List of things.

EDIE DORN: Read it to us, Mister Hammond.

AL HAMMOND: Stale cigarettes. Out-of-date phonebook. Obsolete money. Putrified food. Ad on matchfolder.

ILD: What's all that mean?

PAT: Is that the matchfolder there? (AL HAMMOND *tosses it to her; she reads the ad on it aloud.*) "Amazing opportunity for advancement! To all who can Qualify!" (PAT *stops reading, eyes* AL HAMMOND.) What's the significance of this?

AL HAMMOND: Finish reading it.

PAT: "Mister Glen Runciter"—(*Again* PAT *stops, this time staring at* AL HAMMOND, *then resumes.*)

"Mr. Glen Runciter of the Beloved Brethren Moratorium of Zurich, Switzerland, doubled his income within a week of receiving our free shoe kit with detailed information as to how you also can sell our . . .

Another "Andy Warhol" manifestation of the graphic drawing of the spraycan superimposes, without warning. No sound. Its label reads:

COULD IT BE THAT I HAVE BAD BREATH, TOM? WELL, ED, IF YOU'RE WORRIED ABOUT THAT, TRY TODAY'S NEW UBIK, WITH POWERFUL GERMICIDAL FOAMING

ACTION, GUARANTEED SAFE WHEN TAKEN AS DIRECTED.

The spraycan manifestation vanishes, and the scene, with no time lapse, continues uninterrupted.

PAT: . . . authentic simulated-leather—" (*Again* PAT *ceases reading; this time she laughs.*) "Authentic simulated-leather?" That's funny.

AL HAMMOND: It's not funny. Finish it.

PAT: " . . . loafers to friends, business associates. Mister Runciter, although helplessly frozen in cold-pac, earned four hundred—" (PAT *sets the match folder down on the table.*) Al, did you have this printed up as a gag?

AL HAMMOND: Maybe Runciter had it printed up as a gag.

EDIE DORN: Then you didn't.

AL HAMMOND *seizes the phone, dials. Pause.*

AL HAMMOND: Herr Vogelsang?

HERBERT's *face appears on the phone's viewscreen.*

HERBERT: Have you come to us, sir, in your hour of grief, perhaps to—

AL HAMMOND: This is Runciter Associates in New York. You're still trying to get a protophason signal from Mister Runciter? Have you had any success? Anything at all?

HERBERT: My friends, the hour of long shadows settles finally over all. This is not man's will but God's.

AL HAMMOND: You haven't picked up anything.

HERBERT: No brain activity of any sort, no. But as is our policy, as defined by our iron-clad contract, we will continue to try for a period of one full week.

DON DENNY: At our expense, of course.

ILD: The dead have all the luck. I mean—you can't bill them.

SAMMY MUNDO: You can bill them, but they're very slow in paying.

ILD: On Judgment Day, do they read you your sins in alphabetical order? Or in order of severity?

AL HAMMOND: Are you kidding about all this?

ILD: I—just feel sort of bad.

AL HAMMOND: They cross-reference them. Hang in there, kid. It could have been worse.

TITO APOSTOS: I think they throw your sins all over you from a barrel, like a pickel barrel.

FRED ZAFSKY: You know, I think when I die—I mean after half-life and I'm completely dead, the way Mister Runciter is—the first thing the Recording Angel will say to me is: So this is the little boy who stole the Flexie.

SAMMY MUNDO: What's a flexie?

FRED ZAFSKY: Never mind. It was before your time. Like a sled but with wheels.

FRANCY SPANISH: Where'd you steal that?

TIPPY JACKSON: Is there still any possibility they might pick up a signal from him?

AL HAMMOND: Not really. Not now.

TIPPY JACKSON: Then they're just wasting our money—the organization's money.

WAYLES: I'll determine that. In Mister Chip's absence.

PAT: Then you'll be determining it forever, because on his own Joe Chip will not get back here. He is probably walking around and around his hotel room, wondering how to get out.

AL HAMMOND: (*Reluctantly*) He's not alone. Wendy's with him. I sent her there—to look after him.

PAT: Oh really?

AL HAMMOND: Yes, really. So he will be back.

PAT: I wondered where Miss Perfect was.

DON DENNY: How long have you had that match folder?

AL HAMMOND: A week.

DON DENNY: Was the ad on it?

AL HAMMOND: I never noticed until today, so what do I know? Who can say?

DON DENNY: Nobody can. What do you think, Al? A gag by Runciter? Did he have it printed up before his death? Or Hollis, maybe? As a sort of grotesque joke, knowing he was going to kill Runciter? That by the time we noticed the match folder, Runciter would be in cold-pac, in Zurich, like the match folder says?

SAMMY MUNDO: How would Hollis know we'd take Runciter to Zurich? And not to a moratorium in say New York?

DON DENNY: Because Ella's there.

AL HAMMOND: There's an address on the match folder.

PAT: (*Reading it*) Des Moines, Iowa. *Des Moines, Iowa?* Des Moines???

AL HAMMOND: Yeah, you send to a box number there for your free shoe kit.

ILD: Who needs a free shoe kit?

AL HAMMOND: I was thinking more of a free Runciter Kit. I mean, suppose I write to this box number.

DON DENNY: You're talking about making contact with Runciter.

AL HAMMOND: Well, the moratorium—(AL HAMMOND *breaks off, ponders.*) The only problem here is the stupidity factor. This is not how you establish contact with someone who's died—not by writing to a box number you read off an ad on a match folder. Especially a match folder you've been carrying around five or six days before the man died.

FRED ZAFSKY: Mister Hammond, whose head—I mean, it's Walt Disney's head that's supposed to be on the fifty-cent piece, isn't it?

AL HAMMOND: Disney's or Fidel Castro's. Let's see it.

The coin is passed to him; several others along the way take a good look at it.

PAT: Another obsolete coin.

AL HAMMOND: (*Pan up starkly on coin; we see* RUNCITER*'s embossed profile and simultaneously, we hear* AL HAMMOND*'s voice.*) Runciter! This isn't obsolete; it's just . . .

Now, without being told to, every person in the room systematically goes through his wallet, pockets or purse; all the coins and paper

UBIK: The Screenplay

money are brought out and examined, in silence. Then:

ILD: I have a five poscred note, with a beautiful steel-engraving portrait of Mister Runciter. The rest—they're normal; they're okay. You want to see the five poscred-note, Mister Hammond? But if I give it to you I want to be sure I get it back.

AL HAMMOND: Who else? (*Six hands in the room go up.*) That makes eight of us who've got what I guess we should call "Runciter money," now. Probably by the end of the day it'll all be Runciter money, or in two days. Anyhow, Runciter money will work; it'll start coin-operated machines and appliances and the clerks will accept it and we can pay our debts with it.

DON DENNY: I don't see why the banks should honor this stuff; the government didn't put it out. It's funny money. It's not real.

AL HAMMOND: But the real question is, what does it mean? Not whether the goddam banks'll accept it.

ILD: I see two processes at work. The first of decay, Mister Hammond. Clotted milk and obsolete phonebooks and coins and dehydrated cigarettes; those are manifestations of a backward-going process. But Runciter money isn't a decay process; this is a totally different process, a coming-into-existence, of something that never was before.

EDIE DORN: Wish fulfillment. Maybe Runciter always wanted to have his portrait on legal tender, on all our money, including metal coins. It's grandiose—a great honor.

AL HAMMOND: But matchfolders?

EDIE DORN: Well, I guess not that.

WAYLES: Runciter Associates has traditionally advertised, on TV and in the 'papes and mags, the class media. But Glen Runciter was never directly involved with that; our PR department handles that, and certainly we never have gone into matchfolders. And no organization with class goes into matchfolders; that's like junk mail—that's the trash of the gutter. Glen Runciter would never under any circumstances involve himself with throwaway trash; he was a man of character.

SAMMY MUNDO: He must be doing it just for a gag. (*They all stare at him, as the import sinks in.*) I mean—if he's doing it. Or did it before he died. Ever did it at all. Then or now. I mean, a man like that... (*The door opens. There stands* JOE CHIP,

Philip K. Dick

careworn, drooping.)

CHIP: Write out a check for the ship. It's on the roof. I don't have enough money to pay for it.

WAYLES: I'll settle with the ship, Mister Chip.

CHIP: Al, come with me.

AL HAMMOND *and* JOE CHIP *leave the conference room.*

20.

Separate office, JOE CHIP *and* AL HAMMOND. CHIP *holds briefcase.*

CHIP: The ship fed me tranquilizers the whole way here. So the bill'll be high.

AL HAMMOND: We can sell off one of our subsidiaries. What's in the briefcase and where's Wendy?

CHIP: Yes to both questions. You don't want to see in the briefcase.

AL HAMMOND: You brought me in here to show me, didn't you?

CHIP *clumsily opens briefcase, shows* AL HAMMOND *the dried-out remains of* WENDY *which we previously saw him encounter in the closet of his hotel room.* AL HAMMOND *stares and stares, then beings to laugh.*

AL HAMMOND: Lord god!

CHIP: After I found it—her—in my hotel room closet—

AL HAMMOND: How'd she get there?

CHIP: I talked to some of the hotel employees. Evidently it happened to her early, before she even reached my room. We found bits of cloth in the corridor, leading to my door. But she must have been all right, or nearly all right, when she crossed the lobby; anyhow, nobody noticed anything. And in a big hotel like that they keep somebody or some kind of scanning system watching. And the fact that she managed to reach my room at all . . .

AL HAMMOND: Yeah, that indicates she must have been at least able to walk.

Another "Andy Warhol" graphic representation of the spraycan superimposes, now; the label reads, with the sound of AL

FRIENDS, THIS IS CLEAN-UP TIME AND WE'RE DISCOUNTING ALL OUR SILENT, ELECTRIC UBIKS BY THIS MUCH MONEY. YES, WE'RE THROWING AWAY THE BLUEBOOK. AND REMEMBER: EVERY UBIK ON OUR LOT HAS BEEN USED ONLY AS DIRECTED.

UBIK: The Screenplay

HAMMOND's *and* JOE CHIP's *voices continuing uninterrupted:*

FRIENDS, THIS IS CLEAN-UP TIME AND WE'RE DISCOUNTING ALL OUR SILENT, ELECTRIC UBIKS BY THIS MUCH MONEY. YES, WE'RE THROWING AWAY THE BLUEBOOK. AND REMEMBER; EVERY UBIK ON OUR LOTS HAS BEEN USED ONLY AS DIRECTED.

The manifestation vanishes; scene as before.

CHIP: I'm thinking about the rest of us.

AL HAMMOND: In what way?

CHIP: The same thing. Happening to us.

AL HAMMOND: How could it?

CHIP: (*Angrily*) How could it happen to her? Because of the blast. Radioactivity—delayed degeneration from bombardment by high-energy particles. We're going to wind up like this one by one. Until none of us are left. Until each of us is ten pounds of skin and hair in a plastic bag, with a few dried-up bones thrown in.

AL HAMMOND: All right, there's some force producing rapid decay.

CHIP: Yeah, I think you can say that. It's been at work since the blast on Luna. We already knew that.

AL HAMMOND: But there's another force, a counter-force, moving things in an opposite direction.

CHIP: Oh, there is? Really?

AL HAMMOND: Connected with Runciter. Our money is beginning to have his picture on it. A matchfolder.

CHIP: He was on my vidphone. At the hotel.

AL HAMMOND: On it how?

CHIP: Not on the screen; only his voice.

AL HAMMOND: What did he say?

CHIP: Nothing in particular.

AL HAMMOND: (*Stares at him, slams his right fist savagely into his left palm.*) Okay, could he hear you?

CHIP: Nope. I tried to get through. It was one-way entirely; I was patched in, listening; that was all.

AL HAMMOND: I'd ask you about your money, but that's dumb.

CHIP: What's there to ask? I was going to ask Wayles in there about the larger salary I'm supposed to get now.

AL HAMMOND: Hey man, you know what I'm going to do? Turn on the television.

CHIP: I think we ought to—

AL HAMMOND: We've got to establish contact with him. Two-way contact.

CHIP: You can't do that with the television. You can't talk back to it, whether it's Runciter or some lady with huge boobs. All you get to do is sit and watch.

AL HAMMOND: Don't tell me you've tried.

CHIP: You want to try now, don't you?

AL HAMMOND: (*Pondering*) Did anyone else hear him on your phone? At the hotel?

CHIP: No.

AL HAMMOND: I'd feel better if they had. Then I'd know it wasn't a hallucination on your part.

CHIP: He's not dead.

AL HAMMOND: We lugged his body from Luna to Zurich! You had hold of it yourself!

CHIP: He must not have been in it.

AL HAMMOND: What does that mean?

CHIP: If you think it's a hallucination, let's take the coins, the money you said has his picture on it, and spend it.

AL HAMMOND: (*Laughing*) That's the Joe Chip test for reality: you see if people will accept your money.

CHIP: We should pick a place at random. Outside any hallucinatory construct we might jointly have conjured up due to the trauma of the Lunar blast.

AL HAMMOND *points dramatically at* JOE CHIP, *who points dramatically back at him; their faces show they've got it.*

UBIK: The Screenplay

AL HAMMOND: Baltimore!

CHIP: A supermarket.

AL HAMMOND: A supermarket in Baltimore!

CHIP: Right! We'll go in and make random samplings of what they have. How much Runciter money is there?

AL HAMMOND: (*Yelling*) You just want to cadge all the money!

CHIP: No, I want to try it out on reality! See if it spends!

AL HAMMOND *and* JOE CHIP *glare silently at each other for a time.*

AL HAMMOND: (*More quietly*) We better get it done as quickly as possible and get back here. It's better if we don't get separated from now on. Just to be safe.

Camera pans up on the dried remains of WENDY *which lie on the desk near the two men.*

21.

The Lucky People Supermarket. Totally computerized, with products punched-out-for on a variety of control panels, as if one is at a "Star Trek Command Module." There is a sample of each item behind a glass window, which may remind us of the people in cold-pac. Several uniformed soldiers can be seen prowling with semi-automatic weapons, to protect the valuable food. The shoppers take them for granted. Briefly we catch a glimpse of services offered by this supermarket of tomorrow which our own lack: a psychiatry section; legal representation; guns; bail bonds; sex changes—all by electronic constructs which you pay in advance. AL HAMMOND *and* JOE CHIP *head for the cigarette section.*

AL HAMMOND: Get a pack of Pall Malls.

CHIP: Wings are cheaper.

AL HAMMOND: They don't make Wings any more. They haven't for years.

CHIP: They just don't advertise. It's an honest cigarette that claims nothing.

CHIP *punches appropriate button.*

CIGARETTE MACHINE: Ninety-five cents, please.

Philip K. Dick

AL HAMMOND: Here's a ten poscred bill.

AL HAMMOND *places the paper money within the machine's input drawer; the machine whirrs. During this,* JOE CHIP *is gazing meditatively at a group of giggling girls clustered around a "take your own photo" type booth which is marked* FIVE MINUTE ABORTION—READ INSTRUCTIONS CAREFULLY BEFORE INSERTING COINS. MUST HAVE EXACT CHANGE. NO REFUNDS. *It's obvious* CHIP *is repelled, although fascinated. The girls are pooling their change.* CHIP *turns away.*

CIGARETTE MACHINE: Your change, sir. Please move along. Others are waiting.

From the change slot of the CIGARETTE MACHINE *paper money and coins spill;* AL HAMMOND *collects them; he and* CHIP *then fish out the pack of cigarettes and look at each other.*

AL HAMMOND: It scanned the Runciter bill and found it satisfactory. Could a bill-scanning machine be wrong? No more precise mechanism exists.

AL HAMMOND *ceases talking as* CHIP *tears open the cigarette pack. Shreds of paper and flakes rain down from* CHIP's *fingers.*

CHIP: Stale.

AL HAMMOND: If it'd been Pall Malls it'd prove something. I told you to get Pall Malls.

CHIP: Okay, let's buy a carton of Dominoes. They're the same price as Wings.

AL HAMMOND: Christ, don't pick an offbrand; pick something like Winstons.

CHIP: Kools.

AL HAMMOND: Okay, for god's sake, Kools! (*They purchase a carton of Kools. It slides from the slot;* AL HAMMOND *picks it up, shakes it.*)

It's empty. I can tell by the weight. (AL HAMMOND *breaks open the cigarette carton.*)

But something's in it; I can hear it rattling around.

He holds the opened carton toward CHIP. *Camera pans in. Only a small folded piece of paper: no packs of cigarettes.* AL HAMMOND *unfolds the note. The opened, creased piece of paper now superimposes itself over the screen, blotting out everything the way*

UBIK: The Screenplay

the "Andy Warhol" manifestations did, although this close-up could be natural, for the purpose of showing us what the note says. However, the result is nonetheless identical, whatever the intent. Again we are confronted by a piece of written material, although there is no spraycan around it:

> ESSENTIAL I GET IN TOUCH WITH YOU. SITUATION SERIOUS AND CERTAINLY WILL GET MORE SO AS TIME GOES ON. THERE ARE SEVERAL POSSIBLE EXPLANATIONS, WHICH I'LL DISCUSS WITH YOU. ANYHOW, DON'T GIVE UP. I'M SORRY ABOUT WENDY WRIGHT: IN THAT CONNECTION WE DID ALL WE COULD. G.R.

Again we see AL HAMMOND *and* JOE CHIP *standing in the supermarket with the note.*

AL HAMMOND: Random carton of cigarettes. At a random store. In a town picked at random. And we find a note in it directed to us from Glen Runciter. What do the other cartons have in them? The same note? Every cigarette carton in the world?

AL HAMMOND *purchases another carton of cigarettes, punching the brand-selection button at random. The carton slides down the chute; change spews from the money slot;* AL HAMMOND *lifts the carton, shakes it.*

AL HAMMOND: You can tell by the feel it's okay. Full.

They open this carton—which is Viceroy—tear open one of the packs; fragments of dried paper and fibers trickle from their fingers, as before, crumbling away.

CHIP: How'd he know we'd come here?

AL HAMMOND: Joe, they're dried out, too. Decay...(AL HAMMOND *glances around, taking in whole giant supermarket with all its items.*) How far does it go? *Everything* here?

Dissolve. AL HAMMOND *and* JOE CHIP *purchasing tape recorder still in unopened original carton; they are leaving supermarket, passing through turnstile by armed soldier whom they scarcely notice; on top of tape recorder carton is loaf of bread and jar of pickled herring. Soldier examines their claim check, lets them go on; they are too deep in their conversation even to be aware of him.*

Philip K. Dick

CHIP: You want to open it here?

They stand on busy sidewalk, pausing.

AL HAMMOND: I think I already know what we'll find.

Dissolve; back to Runciter Associates offices. This time at:

22.

Electronic shop of Runciter Associates: workbenches and men with test equipment of futuristic kinds. Tape recorder carton is open; tape recorder itself, disassembled, lies spread out on workbench, parts everywhere.

SHOP FOREMAN: I can tell you what's wrong with it. All the rubber's worn. The drive-tire's got flat spots on it, from wear. It needs a complete overhaul, lubrication, cleaning, including new belts. Frankly, it's not worth it, though. It has seen plenty of use.

AL HAMMOND: "Plenty of use"?

SHOP FOREMAN: Several years, hasn't it?

AL HAMMOND: I bought it today. (*Turns to* JOE CHIP) Brand-new tape recorder completely worn out, bought with funny money. Worthless money, worthless article purchased; has a sort of logic to it.

SHOP FOREMAN: I'll tell you something else about your tape recorder you don't know, I bet. It isn't just worn out; it's forty years behind times. They don't use rubber drive-tires any longer, or belt-run transports. You'll never find parts for it unless someone hand-makes them. I'd forget it.

Dissolve.

23.

JOE CHIP *seated at small table, on which is plastic bowl, carton of milk, box of Alphabets breakfast cereal, shaker of sugar, napkin and spoon. We hear loudly the Verdi "Requiem" again, the "Dies Irae" section.* JOE CHIP *opens cereal box and pours cereal into bowl; pours milk, then sugar onto it. Sits. Only sound that of "Requiem." Pan up of bowl, which shows smooth surface of white milk. Then bits of cereal, which are in the form of letters, float one by one to the surface. One here, one there, with spaces in between.*

UBIK: The Screenplay

We can presently make out portions of incomplete words. Then, finally, the "remaining" alphabet bits float up and the words are completed. They read: HAVING A WONDERFUL TIME, WISH YOU WERE HERE.

Spoon is lowered, and JOE CHIP *begins to consume the milk and cereal. Dissolve.*

24.

Early-evening street; AL HAMMOND *and* JOE CHIP *walking together through the lengthening shadows. Trash, wind-swept, swirls from the gutter and around their twin figures. Camera long shot.*

AL HAMMOND: "Here" must be Des Moines. Who gets to go?

Interval of silence as they slowly walk.

CHIP: I'll go. I've never seen Des Moines.

AL HAMMOND: If you hadn't eaten up the bowl of cereal . . .

CHIP: Don't you believe me about that either?

AL HAMMOND: I believe you. I just wish you had left it long enough for us to photograph it.

CHIP: I was hungry. Anyhow, that's what it said. How can you have a wonderful time in Des Moines, Iowa? Especially if you're dead. And—he's dead in Zurich anyhow, not in Des Moines.

AL HAMMOND: If you're dead I guess you're dead everywhere at once equally. I guess it doesn't matter. But the matchfolder said Des Moines. That's the best clue we have.

CHIP: Why can't we keep pouring bowls of Alphabets cereal? We could have our electronics experts hook a computer in so that every word-formation that swam to the surface of the bowl was stored in memory banks and analyzed for—

AL HAMMOND: Runciter was born in Des Moines. I looked it up.

CHIP: You realize eventually if enough bowls of Alphabets were poured, and the computers built up and then analyzed enough of their memory banks, and enough time passed, that all the information there is would eventually be available to us?

AL HAMMOND: About what?

Philip K. Dick

CHIP: About everything. But you have to figure in the cost of the cereal.

They fade off into the gathering gloom, two tiny figures walking.

25.

Runciter Associates building again, in New York. AL HAMMOND *and* JOE CHIP, *waiting in hall for elevator.*

AL HAMMOND: If we don't get to Des Moines soon . . .

CHIP: Okay, I'll leave tonight. As soon as we tell the others. Why was Runciter born in Des Moines? If you select the womb you're going to enter, he'd know the womb was located in Des Moines. That doesn't show very good planning. That doesn't sound like the Glen Runciter I knew. Are you sure about that? Where'd you look it up, on a gum wrapper?

The elevator arrives. Although the hall was futuristic, the elevator is the circa 1900 open cage kind, with polished brass fittings, suspended from a cable. A dull-eyed uniformed operator sits on a stool, working a wooden handle. AL HAMMOND *starts to get in;* CHIP, *dumbfounded, holds back.*

CHIP: Don't get in, Al.

AL HAMMOND: What's the matter?

CHIP: Look at this elevator and think. Try to remember the elevator we rode in earlier today. Every day, here. The hydraulic-powered, closed, self-operating, absolutely silent . . .

CHIP *ceases talking, because the elderly clanking open-cage elevator has faded into the usual futuristic one of which he is speaking. So he gets in, then, along with* AL HAMMOND. *The doors shut after them.*

AL HAMMOND: Why'd you tell me not to get in?

CHIP: Didn't you see the old elevator?

AL HAMMOND: No.

CHIP: Did you see *anything*?

AL HAMMOND: This. What we're in.

CHIP: Do you feel cold?

AL HAMMOND: No.

UBIK: The Screenplay

CHIP: I feel cold. I feel tired, too.

AL HAMMOND: Too many hours in the sack with your new mistress.

CHIP: My what?

AL HAMMOND: Pat.

CHIP: I think it's the flu.

AL HAMMOND: I think you're depressed by Glen Runciter's death.

CHIP: Yeah, little things depress me. It's symptomatic of something. Then when the big things happen I'm primed to collapse. It's my "will to fail."

The elevator doors open; they exeunt into upper floor hall. JOE CHIP *heads off in opposite direction from* AL HAMMOND.

CHIP: You go on ahead and tell the others about my pilgrimage to Des Moines. And get Wayles to make out a pay voucher in advance so I'm adequately funded.

AL HAMMOND: Where are you going?

CHIP: Can I go to the men's room? I'm going to stay there until I'm adequately funded.

The camera follows AL HAMMOND *as he moves toward conference room; he pauses, looking back at* JOE CHIP *who meanders with obvious weariness toward the men's room.* AL HAMMOND *continues to watch until the men's room door shuts after* JOE CHIP; *then, reluctantly, he starts on. However, the men's room door flies open again immediately; there stands* JOE CHIP, *pale and stricken.*

CHIP: Al! Come here!

AL HAMMOND *hurries toward him; together they enter men's room.* JOE CHIP *points above the urinals. We see this graffiti:* JUMP IN THE URINAL AND STAND ON YOU HEAD./I'M THE ONE THAT'S ALIVE. YOU'RE ALL DEAD.

AL HAMMOND: Is it Runciter's writing? Do you recognize it?

CHIP: It's Runciter's writing.

AL HAMMOND: So now we know the truth.

CHIP: The truth? That's the truth? What a hell of a way to learn it—from the wall of a bathroom, a public bathroom.

Philip K. Dick

AL HAMMOND: That's graffiti for you—harsh and direct. The wisdom of the world. Distilled, simple—we might have watched the television and listened to the vidphones and read the 'papes for months—forever, maybe—without finding out. Without being told straight to the point like this.

CHIP: But we're not dead! Except for Wendy.

AL HAMMOND: We're in half-life. Probably still on the ship, on *Pratfall Two* on our way back to Earth from Luna.

AL HAMMOND, *panting, sits down on one of the toilets, trembling.*

CHIP: You okay?

AL HAMMOND: Sure, sure. We're on our way back, man, after the explosion killed us—killed us, not Runciter. And he's trying to pick up the flow of protophasons from us. But so far he's failed; we're not getting across from our world to his. But he's managed to reach us. We are picking him up, in a fashion. (AL HAMMOND *speaks with greater and greater difficulty, as if losing strength.*) Everywhere. Even places we choose at random. He surfaces in freak ways, at the edge of things—like the matchfolder. His presence is invading us on every . . .

Again an "Andy Warhol" graphic of the spraycan superimposes; the sound cuts off. This time the printing on the label reads:

POP TASTY UBIK INTO YOUR TOASTER, MADE ONLY FROM FRESH FRUIT AND HEALTHFUL ALL-VEGETABLE SHORTENING. UBIK MAKES BREAKFAST A FEAST, PUTS ZING INTO YOUR THING! SAFE WHEN HANDLED AS DIRECTED.

The spraycan graphic vanishes; former scene again, but there has been a transformation: AL HAMMOND *appears frosted-over, silvered with particles of ice; and, as he laboriously breathes, his breath is visible. He has an aged quality, as if centuries have passed.*

AL HAMMOND: . . . side, him and only him because he's the sole person trying to establish—

CHIP: (*Interrupting in agitation*) Al, you look dreadful. You look like hell warmed over. You look a thousand years old, sitting there on that toilet. What is it?

UBIK: The Screenplay

AL HAMMOND: I'm sick.

AL HAMMOND *makes his way totteringly to the wash basin, begins splashing water onto his face; at first the water steams, obviously hot, but then ice forms, cracking and splintering.*

AL HAMMOND: You better go back to the conference room. I'll be along when I feel better, assuming I ever do feel better.

CHIP: I ought to stay here with you.

AL HAMMOND: (*Shouting*) No, goddam it—*get out of here!* (AL HAMMOND *shoves him toward the door of the men's room out into the corridor.*)

Go on; make sure they're all right. You're in charge of them, now; you have to take care of them.

CHIP: Okay, I'll be down the hall in the conference room with them. (*The door of the men's room closes between* JOE CHIP *and* AL HAMMOND.) Al? I want to see with my own eyes that you're all right.

JOE CHIP *pushes open the door. The men's room is entirely dark; we and* JOE CHIP *see nothing. No sign of* AL HAMMOND *within.*

AL HAMMOND: (*Voice alone*) It's too late, Joe. Don't look. You can't do anything to help me anyhow. We shouldn't have separated from the others; that's why it happened to Wendy. You can stay alive at least for a while if you go find them and stick with them constantly. Tell them that; make sure all of them understand. Do you understand?

JOE CHIP *gropes for the light switch. Something strikes against him that bobs weightlessly, like black tumbleweed; he recoils a little and then, with realization that it is* AL HAMMOND *draws back.*

CHIP: I'll go join the others. Yes, I understand. Does it feel very bad?

AL HAMMOND: (*Voice alone, weakly*) No, it doesn't feel very bad. I just—

AL HAMMOND's *voice fades out entirely.*

CHIP: Maybe I'll see you again sometime. (*Pauses, stands there facing the blackness and silence*) Let me put it another way. I hope you feel better. I'll check back after I tell them about the writing on the wall in there. I'll tell them not to come in, though, and look at it because it might—they might bother you. In your condition. Well, so long.

Philip K. Dick

JOE CHIP *goes slowly down hall to conference room. Opening door, he discovers an empty room; but, in progress, a hologram television transmission. The big, expensive company-owned television set shows this on its 3-D screeen: a housewife critically inspecting a towel and in a penetrating, critical typical television commercial voice she says:*

TV HOUSEWIFE: I washed this towel in ordinary synthetic detergents, when I could have gotten the real thing! And look at this bra! (*Television screen cuts to view of* TV HOUSEWIFE*'s bathroom*) But with this new all-purpose cleaner, even grimy walls have that fresh look! Used as directed, you'll find that overnight your conapt will sparkle as never before!

On television screen, the wall of TV HOUSEWIFE*'s bathroom shows graffiti, which she is merrily wiping away by spraying cleaner from spraycan and rubbing with the towel. In the same handwriting as* JOE CHIP *saw in the men's room, the graffiti reads:* LEAN OVER THE BOWL AND THEN TAKE A DIVE. / ALL OF YOU ARE DEAD, I AM ALIVE.

CHIP: Where the hell is everybody? (*Glances around*)

TV HOUSEWIFE: See how this childish ugly scribbling comes right off with just a gentle whisk?

TV HOUSEWIFE *rubs vigorously at the graffiti and it does not come off in the slightest, but she continues to smile into the camera lens.*

CHIP: Scrub harder, lady.

Scrubbing in vain, the TV HOUSEWIFE *looks more and more nervous.* JOE CHIP *goes to control panel and changes channels.*

TV NEWSCASTER: (*Face visible in TV hologram*) And now, back to the news. Glen Runciter came home today to the place of his birth, but it was not the kind of return which gladdened anyone's heart. Yesterday tragedy struck at Runciter Associates, probably the best-known of Earth's many prudence organizations. In a terrorist blast at an undisclosed installation on Luna, Glen Runciter was mortally wounded and died before his remains could be transferred to cold-pac. Flown to the Beloved Brethren Moratorium in Zurich, every effort possible was made in a frantic last-minute effort to revive Runciter to half-life, but in vain. In acknowledgment of defeat these efforts have now ceased, and the body of Glen Runciter has been returned here to Des Moines, where it will lie in state at the Simple Shepherd Mortuary. (*Television* *hologram shows simple white New England style building.*)

It was the sad but inexorably dictated decision by the wife of Glen Runciter which brought about this final chapter which we are now viewing. Mrs. Ella Runciter, herself in cold-pac, whom it had been hoped her husband would join—revived to face this calamity, Mrs. Runciter learned this morning of the fate which had overtaken her husband, and gave the decision to abandon efforts to awaken belated half-life in the man whom she had expected to merge with, a hope disappointed by reality. (*Television hologram shows still photo of ELLA.*)

In solemn ritual, grieving employees of Runciter Associates assembled in the chapel of the Simple Shepherd Mortuary, preparing themselves as best they could, under the circumstances, to pay their respects.

Television hologram shows parked hovership; INTERVIEWER *with microphone is interviewing* DON DENNY.

INTERVIEWER: Tell me, sir, in addition to working for Glen Runciter, did you and your fellow employees also know him as a man?

DON DENNY: We all knew Glen as a man, as a good individual and boss and citizen whom we could trust. I know I speak for the others here when I say this.

INTERVIEWER: Are all of Mister Runciter's employees, or perhaps I should say former employees, here, Mister Denny?

DON DENNY: We're missing a few. I refer in particular to inertials Al Hammond and Wendy Wright and the firm's field tester, Mister Chip. The whereabouts of the three of them is unknown to us, but perhaps along with—

INTERVIEWER: Yes, perhaps they will see this telecast, which is being beamed by satellite over all of Earth, and will make their way here to Des Moines for this tragic occasion *as I'm sure Mister Runciter would want them to.* And now this message.

Television hologram switches to commercial, after a moment of phosphorescent colors and modern abstract-painting-like graphics which flit by at great velocity. The commercial shows an elegantly-furnished office; behind a huge desk sits an older man in solemn repose, about to deliver a serious message. It is GLEN RUNCITER.

RUNCITER: Tired of lazy tastebuds? Has boiled cabbage taken over your world of food? That same old, stale, flat, Monday-

Philip K. Dick

morning odor no matter how many dimes you put into your stove? Ubik changes all that; Ubik wakes up food flavor, puts hearty taste back where it belongs, and restores fine food smell. (*On the Television hologram a brightly colored spraycan replaces* RUNCITER.)

One invisible puff-puff whisk of economically priced Ubik banishes compulsive obsessive fears that the entire world is turning into clotted milk, worn-out tape recorders and obsolete iron-cage elevators, plus other, further, as-yet-unglimpsed manifestations of decay. You see, world deterioration of this regressive type is a normal experience of many half-lifers, especially in the early stages when ties to the real reality still are very strong. A sort of lingering universe is retained as a residual charge, experienced as a pseudo environment but highly unstable and unsupported by any ergic substructure. This is particularly true when several memory systems are fused, as in the case of you people. But with today's new, more-powerful-than-ever Ubik, all this is changed!

On the television hologram screen a cartoon fairy darts about, squirting Ubik here and there, like magic mist.

CHIP: Uh, hey, Glen . . .

The cartoon fairy on the television hologram is replaced by a huge hard-eyed housewife with big teeth and horse's chin; her voice is brassy and obnoxious.

OBNOXIOUS HOUSEWIFE: I came over to Ubik after trying weak, out-of-date reality supports. My pots and pans were turning into heaps of rust. The floors of my conapt were sagging. My husband Charley put his foot right through the bedroom door. But now I use economical new powerful today's Ubik, and with miraculous results. Look at this refrigerator. (*On the television hologram appears an antique, circa 1930, turret-top G.E. refrigerator.*) Why, it devolved back eighty years!

CHIP: Sixty.

OBNOXIOUS HOUSEWIFE: But now look at it.

She squirts the old turret top refrigerator with her spraycan of Ubik. Sparkles of magic light surround the old appliance in a nimbus, and, in a flash, a modern six-door pay refrigerator replaces it (circa 1992).

RUNCITER: (*He again appears on the Television hologram,* *behind his massive desk*) Yes! By making use of the most advanced techniques of modern-day science, the reversion of matter to earlier forms *can* be reversed, and at a price any conapt owner can afford. Ubik is sold by leading supermarkets throughout Earth. Do not take internally. Keep away from open flame. Do not deviate from printed procedural approaches as expressed on label. So look for it, Joe. Don't just sit there; go out and buy a can of Ubik and spray it all around you night and day.

CHIP: (*Loudly*) You know I'm here. Does that mean you can hear and see me?

RUNCITER: Of course I can't hear and see you. This commercial message is on videotape; I recorded it two weeks ago, specifically twelve days before my death. I knew the bomb—

CHIP: Then you really are dead.

RUNCITER: Of course I'm dead. Didn't you watch the telecast from Des Moines just now?

CHIP: What about the graffiti on the men's room wall?

RUNCITER: Another deterioration phenomenon. Go buy a can of Ubik and it'll stop happening to you; all those things will cease.

CHIP: (*Puzzled*) Al thinks we're dead.

RUNCITER: Al is deteriorating. Look, Joe, I recorded this goddam television commercial—at great expense, incidentally—to assist you, to guide you—you in particular because we've always been friends—do you understand? I knew you'd be very confused, which is exactly what you are right now, totally confused. Which isn't very surprising, considering your usual condition. Anyhow, try to hang in there; maybe once you get to Des Moines and see my body lying in state you'll calm down.

CHIP: What's this "Ubik"?

RUNCITER: I think, though, it's too late to help Al.

CHIP: What is Ubik made of? How does it work?

RUNCITER: As a matter of fact, Al probably induced the writing on the men's room wall. By the ebbing away of himself, the vacuum he created. He drew it into your world.

CHIP: You really are on videotape, aren't you? You can't hear me or see me.

Philip K. Dick

The horse-jawed OBNOXIOUS HOUSEWIFE *reappears on the television hologram.*

OBNOXIOUS HOUSEWIFE: If the supermarket you patronize doesn't yet carry Ubik, return to your conapt, Mister Chip, and you'll find a free sample has arrived by mail, a free introductory sample, Mister Chip, that will keep you going until you can buy a regular size can. That's assuming you ever get hold of some money.

The OBNOXIOUS HOUSEWIFE *fades out. Hologram goes dark.*

CHIP: I will do my best at all times.

26.

The building in which JOE CHIP *lives, as before. He lets himself into his apartment. It is entirely changed—transformed backward into the past. We see appliances which are old-fashioned even to us; none of the futuristic coin-operated ones presented before. Stove is old gas-burner. Toaster isn't even popup type. Refrigerator is ancient belt-driven type.* JOE CHIP *prowls about in a state of shock. His television set has reverted to a wood-cabinet Atwater-Kent AM radio.*

CHIP: (*Filter*) If it's going to revert backward into time, why hasn't the television set reverted to formless metals and plastics? After all, those are its constituents; it was constructed out of them, not out of an earlier radio. Perhaps this verifies an ancient philosophy: Plato's ideal objects, the universals which in each class are real. Prior forms must carry on an invisible, residual life in every object. The past is latent, submerged, but still here, capable of rising to the surface once the later printing, through some unfortunate accident, vanishes. The man contains—not the boy—but earlier men. But didn't Plato think that something survived the decay and decline of forms? Something inside, not able to decay? The body ending, like Wendy did, and the soul—out of its nest the bird, flown elsewhere. To be reborn again, as the Tibetan Book of the Dead says. It really is true. Christ, I hope so. Because then we can all meet again. As in Winnie-the-Pooh, in another part of the forest; perhaps we will all wind up like Pooh, and always be playing, in a clearer, more durable new place. Leaving these frozen, discarded objects behind.

JOE CHIP *turns on the ancient Atwater-Kent radio set.*

UBIK: The Screenplay

RADIO ANNOUNCER: Time for Pepper Young's Family, brought to you by mild Camay, the soap of beautiful women. Yesterday Pepper unexpectedly discovered that the labor of months had come to a shattering end, due to the—

JOE CHIP *shuts off the radio. Continues to wander about his old-time apartment, marveling at the antique objects. On a baroque glass-topped coffee table he examines a copy of* Liberty *magazine. Studies a faded Turkish rug on the hardwood floor. Glances up at a monochrome framed print on the wall of a dying Indian brave on horseback. Comes at last to the telephone: the upright hook type.* CHIP *lifts receiver from hook.*

OPERATOR: (*Filter*) Number, please.

CHIP *hangs up telephone. Goes on, to discover antique gas heater with large tin flu running up wall. Goes from there into bedroom, looks in closet, then brings out and assembles entire 1930's outfit of clothes: black Oxfords, wool socks, knickers, blue cotton shirt, camel's hair sports coat and golf cap. Then, beside this on the bed, he lays out: pin-striped blue-black double-breasted suit, suspenders, wide floral necktie and white shirt with celluloid collar. Rummaging in closet again he drags out huge golf bag with assorted clubs. Now he returns to living room, inspects the crank-handled windup phonograph, lowboy style; picks up ten-inch 78 speed black-label Victor record; we see on label: TURKISH DELIGHT by Ray Noble's Orchestra.* CHIP *puts record on phonograph, winds it up; as it plays, he goes to sofa, seats himself and picks up folded newspaper. Front page:*

FRENCH CLAIM SIEGFRIED LINE DENTED REPORT GAINS IN AREA NEAR SAARBRUCKEN MAJOR BATTLE SAID TO BE SHAPING UP ALONG WESTERN FRONT

CHIP *refolds newspaper to read another item:*

POLISH REPORT CLAIMS GERMAN FORCES HALTED SAY INVADERS THROW NEW FORCES INTO BATTLE WITHOUT NEW GAINS

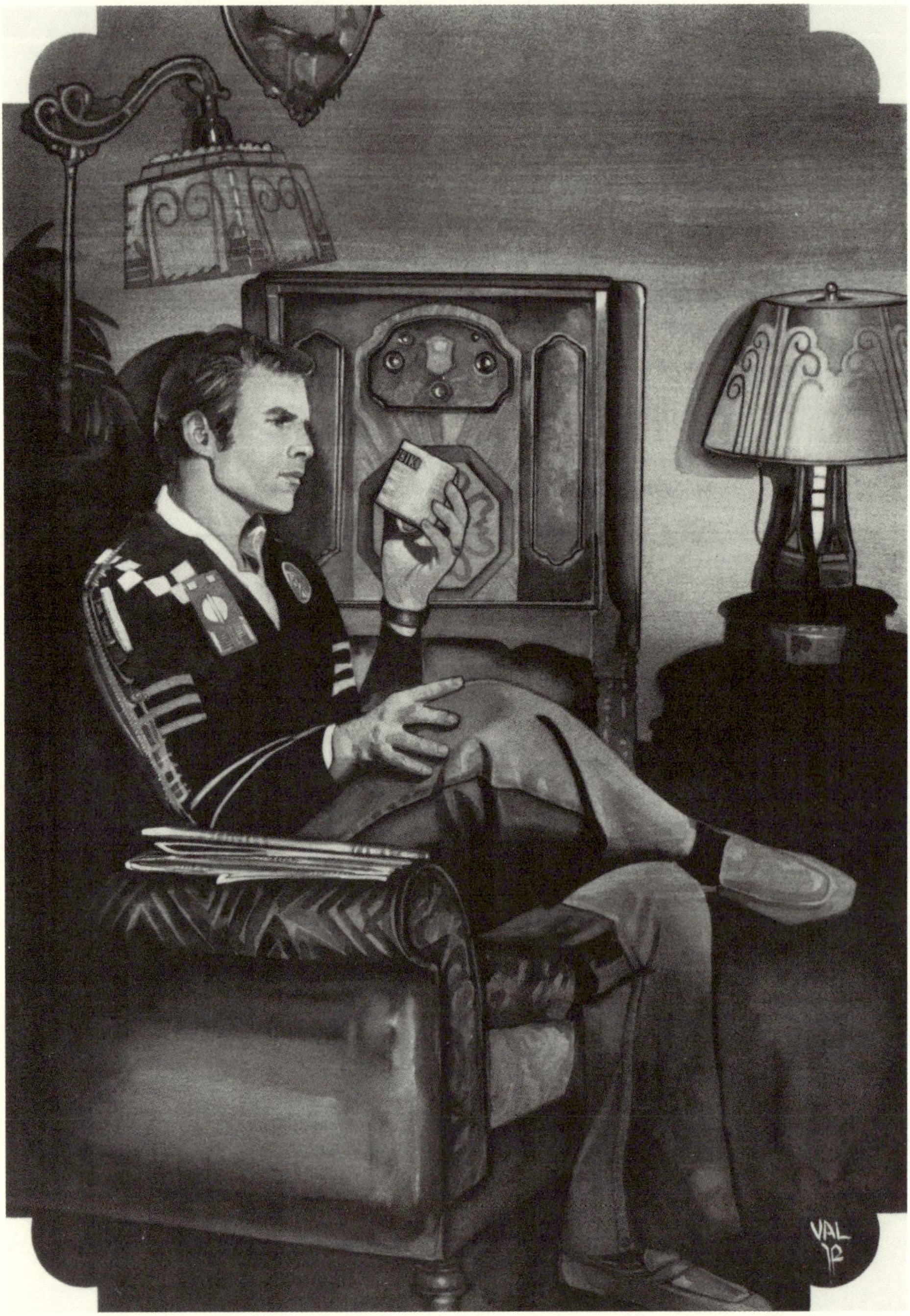

UBIK: The Screenplay

CHIP *folds back newspaper expertly and reads comics page. As if he's always done it. Sitting thus, with the furnishings and other nostalgia objects around him,* CHIP *could, except for his clothes, be an ordinary resident of a 1930's apartment, reading his evening paper. His absorption in his newspaper however is interrupted by a noise: squeak of metal hinge, then light thud.* CHIP *turns his head questioningly, then sets the newspaper down carefully on the sofa and walks toward front door. We see a metal-hinged mail slot; through it has come today's mail. A few letters—and a small brown-wrapped package.* CHIP *picks up the mail, glances over the letters—as if all this is still familiar and ordinary to him—and then studies the package.*

CHIP: (*Filter*) It's the wrong shape for a spraycan. They sent me the wrong thing. Must be a sample of something else. Maybe the shoe kit.

CHIP *unwraps package; finds inside a blue glass jar with a large lid. The label reads: UBIK LIVER AND KIDNEY BALM.*

CHIP: (*Filter*) It's regressed, too. Ubik has regressed; the thing that stops regression. This is insane!

Close up of label, to resemble the "Andy Warhol" manifestations:

"DIRECTIONS FOR USE. This unique analgesic formula, developed over a period of forty years by Dr. Edward Sonderbar, is guaranteed to end forever annoying getting up at night. You will sleep peacefully for the first time, and with superlative comfort. Merely dissolve a teaspoonful of UBIK LIVER AND KIDNEY BALM in a glass of warm water and drink immediately one-half hour before retiring. If pain or irritation persist, increase dosage to one tablespoonful. Do not give to children. Contains processed oleander leaves, saltpeter, oil of peppermint, N-Acetyl-p-aminophenol, zinc oxide, charcoal, cobalt chloride, caffeine, extract of digitalis, steroids in trace amounts, sodium citrate, ascorbic acid, artificial coloring and flavoring. UBIK KIDNEY AND LIVER BALM is potent and effective if handled as per instructions. Inflammable. Use rubber gloves. Do not allow to get in eyes. Do not splash on skin. Do not inhale over long periods of time. Warning: prolonged or excessive use may result in habituation."

CHIP: (*Filter*) This stuff isn't what Runciter advertised on TV. This is some archane mixture of old-time patent medicines, skin

Philip K. Dick

salves, pain killers, poisons, inert nothings—plus of all things, cortisone. Which didn't even exist in this time-period. What do I do now? They're all in Des Moines; they left me behind with the kidney and liver balm. My God—that's what Al said kills you, being left alone. I am a tragic and doomed figure. I better get to Des Moines. What am I doing here in this old apartment? I'm half-way into death. I'm *liking* it. This sample in the mail was a fraud, a snare. A gyp! (CHIP *begins to move swiftly; he is bailing out.*) I wonder what it costs to get to Des Moines.

As he exits from apartment we see him fishing in his pocket for his wallet.

27.

JOE CHIP *walking down outside concrete stairs which have wrought-iron railings, to street. We hear audio commercial, in tinny sound of old-time radio, very loud:*

COMMERCIAL: (*Chorus*) Stand up, stand up, for Jesus' sake!

COMMERCIAL: (*Old-time announcer*) This message brought to you by Preparation U, whose motto is: "It's bitchin' to be itchin'." (*NBC chimes follow*)

JOE CHIP *strides on, hunched over, as if perhaps he, like us, hears this revolting anachronistic plug. Stopping on sidewalk, he looks to left and right. All parked vehicles are from the 1930's. So are the buildings, and the clothing-styles of passers-by. Joe walks up to parked 1939 LaSalle and stands mutely, gazing at it. After an interval he reaches into his pockets, searches, brings out a set of keys. He tries each of the keys until one of them unlocks the door of the LaSalle. Then, getting behind the wheel, he inserts a key into the ignition. The engine starts up.* JOE CHIP *slams the car door shut. We hear the clash of gears. The LaSalle bucks violently, then begins to lurch ahead; obviously, he is unaccustomed to operating the clutch. We see the LaSalle recede off down the 1930's street in that inept fashion, like a fade away in a Laurel and Hardy film.*

28.

An ancient, small airport. Biplanes parked showing huge wooden props. The windsock. A few 1930's type autos parked. Yellow wood slat airport building and parked planes stage front; far off, the LaSalle bucking and lurching, more evenly handled, now, but obviously still driven by a novice—JOE CHIP. *The LaSalle comes closer and closer and at last reaches the dirt section used as a car parking area. Since the autos are all painted black, and the ground is dull brown, and the building dull yellow, there is a peculiar lack of color in this scene. LaSalle halts.* JOE CHIP *emerges, slams and locks car door after him, then with key unlocks car door, reaches inside, brings out the bottle of* UBIK LIVER AND KIDNEY BALM. *Holding it under his right arm he again locks car door; while doing this he manages to drop the bottle onto the ground. It doesn't break. As he bends to pick it up, the LaSalle slowly rolls forward.* JOE CHIP *grabs at the door-handle, but the door is now locked. The car continues to roll. He manages to locate his key and stands there holding it, looking after the car, which now passes from camera range at left.* JOE CHIP *stares in that direction for a time. The sound of a crash. He then restores the key to his pocket, turns and walks in the other direction.*

Two airport guys loafing around, one wearing a train conductor style cap and unbuttoned sweater, gold-rimmed glasses; he is an OFFICIAL. JOE CHIP *approaches them; they watch him, perplexed and amused by his odd clothes.*

CHIP: What can I charter with this?

CHIP *shows them all the money he has. Their smiles broaden.*

OFFICIAL: Hey, Sam. Come here and look at this money.

Individual wearing a striped shirt with billowing sleeves, shiny seersucker trousers and canvas shoes, appears; this is SAM.

SAM: Land o'Goshen. Fake money.

OFFICIAL: No, it's money from the future. Look at the dates.

The three individuals pass JOE CHIP'S *money among them, back and forth.*

SAM: You don't hardly see money from the future these here days.

He laughs. They all laugh. They return JOE CHIP'S *money to him.*

OFFICIAL: I'll tell you what you can charter with this. A hot air balloon.

SAM: We'll provide the balloon and you provide . . .

They all break up laughing.

CHIP: I have a '39 LaSalle parked in the lot. I'll trade it for a one-way flight to Des Moines on any plane that'll get me there. Does that interest you?

Philip K. Dick

OFFICIAL: Maybe Oggie Brent would be interested.

SAM: Brent? You mean that Jenny of his? That airoplane's twenty years old. It wouldn't get to Philadelphia.

OFFICIAL: How about McGee?

SAM: Sure, but he's in Newark.

OFFICIAL: Then maybe Sandy Jespersen. That Curtiss-Wright of his would make it to Iowa. Sooner or later. (*To* JOE CHIP, *pointing.*) Go out by hanger three and look for a red and white Curtiss biplane. You'll see a little short guy, sort of fat, fiddling around with it. If he don't take you up on it nobody here will, unless you want to wait till tomorrow for Ike McGee to come back here in his Fokker trimotor.

CHIP: Thanks.

CHIP *walks until he comes to little short fat man who is puttering with an oily rag at the wheels of a biplane; each man gazes at the other.*

CHIP: You Jespersen?

JESPERSEN: That's my name and that's my game.

CHIP *says nothing for a time; his face shows the pain he is suffering, here in this regressed world; every encounter is a further tribulation. Finally he masters his gloom and speaks.*

CHIP: You want to trade me a one-way trip to Des Moines for a new LaSalle? Even trade?

JESPERSEN: Might as well be both ways. (JESPERSEN *resumes polishing his airoplane.*) I got to fly back here anyway. Okay, I'll take a look at it, but I'm not promising anything; I haven't made up my mind.

Throwing down his rag, JESPERSEN *accompanies* JOE CHIP. *Dissolve to parking area of field. The two men are standing there unmoving, both of them surveying the parked cars. There is no LaSalle.*

CHIP: Gosh.

With JESPERSEN *following,* CHIP *walks over to a small fabric-top Ford coupe—a 1929 flivver. A cheap Model A with eisenglas windows. The front bumper and right front fender are dented; in fact the bumper is merely hanging.* CHIP *stands, then reaches, seizes the bumper and yanks it off the car. Then he kicks the right front tire. Air oozes from the tire at the rear of the car, not the one he kicked. He then grabs hold of the door-handle on the driver's side and yanks. The door on the other side of the car flies off. Walking a few feet off* CHIP *takes aim and runs at the Model A; as he gets close to it, the car's horn beeps pathetically, in fear.* CHIP *halts. The horn wavers into silence.* CHIP *lifts his fist threateningly; the car horn beeps again in fear. Disgusted,* CHIP *turns his back on the worthless car.*

JESPERSEN: (*Uneasily*) Uh, I'll see you later, mister.

CHIP: You don't want the car.

CHIP *opens door on driver's side, gets in and sits down.*

CHIP: (*Filter*) This is it. Like Runciter pointed out in his TV commercial—this means death. The death that came over Wendy and Al. What a place. What a time.

CHIP: (*Speaks to* JESPERSEN) I was hoping to live to see the bombing of Pearl Harbor. And the rape of the Philippines.

JESPERSEN: What's that you got there on the seat beside you?

CHIP *looks, discovers—close up: the bottle of UBIK KIDNEY AND LIVER BALM has regressed; it is now seamless and flat, the kind of handmade bottle produced from a wooden mold. Its label reads:*

> ELIXER OF UBIQUE, GUARANTEED TO RESTORE LOST MANLINESS AND TO BANISH VAPORS OF ALL KNOWN KINDS AS WELL AS TO RELIEVE REPRODUCTIVE COMPLAINTS IN BOTH MEN AND WOMEN. A BENEFICENT AID TO MANKIND WHEN SEDULOUSLY EMPLOYED AS INDICATED.

And in smaller letters below:

> DON'T DO IT, JOE. THERE'S ANOTHER WAY. KEEP TRYING. YOU'LL FIND IT. LOTS OF LUCK.

JESPERSEN: Where'd you get this? They haven't made these—see, scratch marks, from the wooden mold. And the cap's hand-threaded. My grandmother had some of these, from around the Civil War time.

CHIP: I inherited it. Along with the car.

JESPERSEN: Yeah, you must have. The company never put out very many in the first place. This medicine was invented in San Francisco around 1850. Never sold in stores; the customers

Philip K. Dick

    had to order it made up. It came in three strengths. This, what you have here, this is the strongest—

Another "Andy Warhol" manifestation, superimposed; the graphic of the spraycan. No sound. The label reads:

TAKEN AS DIRECTED, UBIK PROVIDES UNINTERRUPTED SLEEP WITHOUT MORNING-AFTER GROGGINESS. YOU AWAKEN FRESH, READY TO TACKLE ALL THOSE LITTLE ANNOYING PROBLEMS FACING YOU. DO NOT EXCEED RECOMMENDED DOSAGE.

Manifestation of spraycan vanishes; previous scene resumes:

JESPERSEN: —of the three. Do you know what's in this?

CHIP: Oil of peppermint, zinc oxide, sodium citrate, charcoal . . .

JESPERSEN: Let it go. I'll fly you to Des Moines in exchange for the flask of Ubique. Let's start her up now; I'm of a mind to do as much flying as possible in daylight.

JESPERSEN *picks up the flask of Ubique, starts off;* CHIP *accompanies him.*

29.

The Curtiss-Wright biplane climbing into the sky; long shot, then dissolve to JOE CHIP *and* JESPERSEN *in helmets and goggles aboard. Noise of engine. They've leveled out.*

CHIP: (*Yelling*) How long will it take to get there?

JESPERSEN: (*Yelling back*) Depends on how much tailwind we get. Hard to say. Probably around noon tomorrow if our luck holds out.

CHIP: (*Yelling*) Will you tell me now what's in the Ubique flask?

JESPERSEN: (*Yelling*) Gold flakes suspended in a base composed mostly of mineral oil.

CHIP: (*Yelling*) How much gold? Very much?

JESPERSEN *turns his head, grins without answering.*

UBIK: The Screenplay

30.

The Curtiss-Wright taxiing to a halt at the Des Moines airport. With no wasted time or motions, JOE CHIP *hurries from plane, across field to airport offices.*

31.

Interior of airport office building: old-fashioned wooden benches, great old wall clock, women in the fashions of the 1930's, men off at a saloon-style bar. This is the Midwest rather than the East Coast: men wear straw hats; the women show less style in their hair, their purses and shoes. More of a rustic quality than those on the sidewalks back in New York, where we saw fur coats. Using the telephone at the ticket counter, JOE CHIP *converses in a hectic, agitated manner.*

CHIP: Hello?

BLISS: (*Filter*) Simple Shepherd Mortuary. Mister Bliss speaking.

CHIP: I'm here to attend the services for Glen Runciter. Am I too late? I say, am I too late?

BLISS: (*Filter*) What's that?

CHIP: (*Loudly*) Am I too late for the services of Mister Glen Runciter?

The airport personnel and the ticket counter people listen to all this with no interest whatsoever, as if graven in stone.

BLISS: (*Filter*) You must be Mister Chip. Services for Mister Runciter are in progress right now.

CHIP: Shit.

BLISS: (*Filter*) Pardon, sir?

CHIP: Then I'm too late?

BLISS: (*Filter*) Where are you, sir? Would you like us to send a vehicle to fetch you?

CHIP: What? To what?

BLISS: (*Filter*) Can you hold the phone closer to your voice, Mister Chip? I can hardly hear you.

CHIP: This is my voice! I'm at the airport!

BLISS: (*Filter*) You really should have arrived earlier, Mister Chip.

Philip K. Dick

> I doubt very much if you'll be able to attend any of the service. However, Mister Runciter will be lying in state for the balance of today and possibly tomorrow, if the weather holds. Is there a Miss Wright with you, Mister Chip?

CHIP: No, she's dead.

BLISS: (*Filter*) A Mister Alvin Hammond?

CHIP: He's dead, too. In the men's room back in New York.

BLISS: (*Filter*) Several of the bereaved have asked that we maintain a vigil for you as well as for Mister Hammond and Miss Wright. You don't happen to know what arrangements have been made regarding Miss Wright and Mister Hammond do you?

CHIP: Like what? No, I don't.

BLISS: (*Filter*) Watch for our car, Mister Chip; it will be there to pick you up shortly. As to the arrangements for Miss Wright and—

JOE CHIP *hangs up. Walks a step back from phone. Behind the ticket counter the elderly clerk now nods toward him.*

CLERK: Mister, come over here a sec.

CHIP: (*Approaching the* CLERK.) What's wrong?

CLERK: This nickel you gave me.

CHIP: It's a buffalo nickel; isn't that the right coin for this period? "If the weather holds." "If the *weather* holds?" I must have reached the point of no return.

CLERK: This nickel is dated 1940. (CHIP *groans, gets out his remaining coins, finds one that will do, gives it to* CLERK.) We get counterfeit money every now and then. Always from persons passing through, from out of town.

CHIP *wanders about waiting room, then notices Western Union counter; he heads for it.*

CHIP: I'd like to send a wire service. (*The* WESTERN UNION MAN *eyes him beadily.*) A wire.

The WESTERN UNION MAN *presents him with the usual pad.* CHIP *begins writing. Time passes. He finishes.* WESTERN UNION MAN *takes pad back, reads* CHIP*'s message aloud:*

WESTERN UNION MAN: "Dear Mister President. The Japanese

will bomb Pearl Harbor on December Seventh 1941 but America will win the war in 1945 because of the Atomic Bomb." (WESTERN UNION MAN *again eyes* CHIP) Who is this to be sent to?

CHIP: Franklin Roosevelt.

WESTERN UNION MAN: That'll be ... (*He counts words in message*) Two-eighty. Two dollars and eighty cents.

CHIP: (*Resting his elbows on counter*) Could you send that collect?

32.

Along Des Moines street slowly moves a 1930 Willys-Knight 87; in it JOE CHIP *and a hempen homespun man dressed in hayseed mourning clothes:* MR. BLISS. *Both men sit bolt upright in front seat.* BLISS *drives. They look very solemn and formal, and very strange: so stiff as to be unreal. Neither takes his eyes from the street directly ahead, during entire following. We get the impression that the car is standing still on a treadmill, and the scenery is being revolved, repeating itself. For example, the same drugstore goes past several times. Also, there seems to be exactly two men sitting together in the front of each of the other vehicles; they gaze straight ahead, like* BLISS *and* CHIP, *and somehow resemble them. All vehicles move at exactly the same speed, as if forming a giant two-way cortege. Also, all vehicles have their headlights turned on. It's a little unnerving.*

BLISS: Care for some Sen-sen?

CHIP: Don't mind if I do.

The little packet of Sen-sen is passed to CHIP; *he partakes.*

BLISS: Unusual line of business that Mister Runciter was in. I'm not certain I quite understand it. For example, what does "psionic" signify? Several of Mister Runciter's employees have made mention of that term.

CHIP: Parapsychological powers. Either netting in knowledge on a direct basis, not through sensory channels, or mental force operating directly, without any intervening physical agency.

BLISS: Mystical powers, you mean? Such as knowing the future? The reason I refer to that, Mister Chip, is that several of you people have made mention about the future in a fashion as to suggest it already exists. Not to me; they didn't impart any mention to me, but I overheard—well, you know how it is. When you're in this business you overhear a lot of things.

CHIP: Like what? You don't have cold-pac here; you don't have half-life. What's there to overhear?

BLISS: I'd be beholden to you, Mister Chip, if you could disclose to me a jot or tittle about the future.

CHIP: As I told President Roosevelt, Japan will attack the U.S. on December 7, 1941.

BLISS: Is that gospel, Mister Chip?

BLISS *honks at red irish setter in street; it dodges and retreats. Other car horns sound, too, virtually in unison.*

CHIP: Bet your boots. However, the U.S. will win in—

BLISS: I mean about your telling President Roosevelt.

CHIP: Yes.

BLISS: You're not in with the Communists, are you?

CHIP: Pardon?

BLISS: There're many Communists in this country, especially back East, around New York. The Communists are the real menace, not the Germans. Take the treatment of the Jews. You know who makes a lot out of that? Jews in this country, plenty of them not even citizens but foreign refugees living on public welfare, at our expense. I think the Nazis certainly have been a little extreme in some of the things they've done to the Jews, but basically there's been the Jewish question for a long time. We have a similar problem here in the U.S. both with Jews and with the niggers. We're going to have to do something about both.

For the first time, CHIP *turns his head and looks directly at* BLISS. *Then* BLISS, *too, turns his head; they gaze silently at each other, and then* CHIP *punches* BLISS *in the eye.* BLISS *blinks, then draws back and punches* CHIP *in the eye.*

CHIP: Racist bigot!

BLISS: How so, Mister Chip?

CHIP: I never actually heard the term "nigger" used before.

BLISS: Touch of the tar brush, Mister Chip?

Once more CHIP *and* BLISS *punch each other out furiously; the Willys-Knight weaves all over the street, as do the other vehicles, oddly; it is total chaos. The solemnity, the slow order of the cortege, is destroyed; horns beep, brakes squeal, drivers curse at one another, cars go up on the sidewalk. Dissolve to the Willys-Knight up against the broken fire hydrant; water spouts out.* BLISS *and* CHIP *sit disgustedly in their car-seats, not stirring.*

CHIP: You're not going to enjoy the next five years.

BLISS: Why not? The whole state of Iowa is behind me in what I say. You know what I think about you employees of Mister Runciter? From what you've said and from what those others said, what I overheard, I think you're professional agitators. That's why you all wear these alien clothes.

The red irish setter which BLISS *previously honked at now runs up to the stalled Willys-Knight, lifts its leg; both* BLISS *and* CHIP *watch with identical expressions of horror as the dog pees on the car.* BLISS *and* CHIP *simultaneously stand up, peer to see the damage. As the dog pees, the water from the hydrant ceases.*

33.

The Simple Shepherd Mortuary: as seen previously on television, the white frame New England building. The group of inertials stand around: EDIE DORN, TIPPY JACKSON, JON ILD, FRANCY SPANISH, TITO APOSTOS, DON DENNY, SAMMY MUNDO, FRED ZAFSKY *and* PAT CONLEY. *All appear depressed, but glance up as a yellow tow truck arrives towing the Willys-Knight. Out of the cab of the tow truck step* BLISS *and* JOE CHIP.

BLISS: Here lies Mister Runciter in perpetuity.

CHIP: I thought we were in Des Moines.

Eying CHIP *with cool distaste,* PAT CONLEY *saunters from the group of inertials toward him.*

PAT: Hi, Joe Chip.

CHIP: Hello. (PAT's *presence has brought him down immediately; his tone is now awkward and nervous; he is ill-at-ease all at once—transformed.*)

Say, are you—are we married? I remember a ring, a silver wedding ring you were wearing, with a stone on it. (CHIP *looks uncertainly toward her left hand.*) You must have changed that. Your last name's "Conley," isn't it?

PAT: I'll discuss it with you some other time.

CHIP: That'd be nice of you.

DON DENNY: No Al Hammond?

CHIP: Al's dead. Wendy Wright is dead.

PAT: We know about Wendy.

DON DENNY: No, we didn't know; we assumed but we weren't sure. *I* wasn't sure. What happened to them? Who killed them?

CHIP: They wore out.

EDIE DORN: Mister Chip, since we came to this place, this town, it has radically changed! None of us understand it. Do you see what we see?

CHIP: I'm not sure what it is you see.

TITO APOSTOS: Come on, Chip; don't mess around; tell us, for chrissakes, what this place looks like to you. That vehicle you were towing. Tell us what it is. It's old; all of this is old.

SAMMY MUNDO: Mister Chip, that's a real antique classic automobile, isn't it? Precisely how old? You can tell us.

CHIP: Sixty-two years old.

TIPPY JACKSON: That would make it 1930. Which is pretty close to what we figured.

DON DENNY: We figured 1939.

CHIP: It's fairly easy to establish that. I took a look at a newspaper at my conapt in New York. September 12th. So today is September 13th, 1939. The French think they've breached the Siegfried Line.

ILD: That is a million laughs, Mister Chip, considering what is about to happen to them.

CHIP: Yeah, everyone here is in for a million laughs, when you look up the time pipe at what's ahead.

FRED ZAFSKY: If it's 1939 it's 1939; there's nothing we can do about it, any more than anyone else can. We should try to make the best of it. Facts are facts. You have to live with them.

CHIP: (*To* PAT) What do you say about this? (PAT *merely shrugs.*)

UBIK: The Screenplay

Don't shrug. Answer.

PAT: We've gone back in time.

CHIP: Not really.

PAT: Then what have we done? Gone forward in time, is that it?

CHIP: We haven't gone anywhere. We're where we've always been. But for some reason—for one of several possible reasons—reality has receded. It's lost its underlying support and it's ebbed back to previous forms. Forms it took fifty-three years ago. Forms we didn't know were still with us underlying our contemporary impressions. It may regress further. I'm more interested, at this point, in knowing if Runciter has manifested himself to you.

DON DENNY: Runciter is lying inside this building in his casket, dead as a herring. That's the only manifestation we've had of him, and that's the only one we're going to get.

FRANCY SPANISH: Does the word "Ubik" mean anything to you, Mister Chip?

CHIP: (CHIP *stares at her, with realization.*) Jesus Christ.

FRANCY SPANISH: No, "Ubik," Mister Chip. I said "Ubik."

CHIP: Can't you tell when you're receiving manifestations from . . .

TIPPY JACKSON: Francy has dreams; she's always had them. Tell him your Ubik dream, Francy. Francy will now tell you her Ubik dream. She had it last night. That's what she calls it; her "Ubik" dream.

FRANCY SPANISH: I call it that because that's what it is. Listen, Mister Chip; it wasn't like any dream I've ever had before. A great hand came—well, it started out, I was standing on a chair, reaching up to a high shelf; there was a package of baking soda on the shelf and I was striving to reach it. Arm and Hammer baking soda. And then out of the drawing came this huge arm and hand, like the hand of you know—God. Enormous; the size of a mountain. And I knew at the time how important it was. The hand was closed, made into a vast fist. And I knew it contained something of value *so great* that my life and the lives of everyone else *on Earth* depended on it. And I waited for the fist to open. And it did open. And I saw what it contained.

DON DENNY: (*Sarcastically*) An aerosol spray can.

FRANCY SPANISH: On the spray can there was one word, great golden letters, glittering; golden fire spelling out UBIK. Nothing else. Just that strange word. And then the hand closed up again around the spray can and the hand-and-arm disappeared, drawn back up into a sort of overcast. Today before the funeral services I looked in a dictionary and I called the public library here, but no one knew that word or even what language it is and it isn't in the dictionary. It isn't English, the librarian told me. There's a Latin word very close to it: *ubique*; it means—

CHIP: "Everywhere."

FRANCY SPANISH: Yes, that's what it means. But no U-b-i-k, the way it was spelled in the dream.

CHIP: They're the same word. Different spellings.

PAT: How do you know that, Joe Chip?

CHIP: Runciter appeared to me yesterday. In a taped television commercial that he made before his death.

PAT: You miserable fool.

CHIP: What?

PAT: Is that your idea of a "manifestation" of a dead man? You might as well consider letters he wrote before his death "manifestations." Or interoffice memos that he taped over the years. Or photographs. Or even—

CHIP: I'm going inside and take a last look at Runciter.

CHIP *walks away from the others, up the wide board steps and into the darkness of the interior of the mortuary. Emptiness and silence. No music. Rows of pew-like seats, dimly visible. Old-fashioned pump organ off in a side alcove, unplayed. Varnished woodwork.* CHIP *walks somberly up the aisle to stand by the big oak casket, to gaze down. Abrupt close up of interior of casket. A dehydrated heap of bones at one end: paper-like skull leering up, eyes recessed like dried grapes. Tatters of cloth with bristle-like woven spines collected near the body, as if blown there by wind.* RUNCITER'*s remains resemble those of* WENDY'*s. Seeing this sight,* CHIP *is visibly stunned.*

CHIP: Well, Glen, I guess—well this is it, then.

CHIP *leaves the casket, makes his way outdoors again. Tears can be seen on his cheeks as he reaches the sunlight and porch.*

UBIK: The Screenplay

DON DENNY: What's the matter?

CHIP: Nothing.

PAT: You look petrified.

CHIP: It's nothing!

TIPPY JACKSON: While you were in there did you by any chance happen to see Edie Dorn?

ILD: She's missing.

CHIP: She was just out here.

DON DENNY: All day she's been saying she felt terribly cold and tired. It may be that she went back to the hotel; she said something about it earlier, that she wanted to lie down and take a nap right after the services. She's probably okay.

CHIP: She's probably dead. (CHIP *looks around at all of them with ferocity; they are surprised.*) I thought you understood. If any of us gets separated from the group he won't survive; what happened to Wendy and Al and Runciter—

CHIP *breaks off.*

DON DENNY: Runciter was killed in the blast.

CHIP: We were all killed in the blast. I know that because Runciter told me. He wrote it on the wall of the men's room back in our New York offices. And I saw it again on—

PAT: What you're saying is insane! Is Runciter dead or isn't he? Are we dead or aren't we? First you say one thing, then you say another. Can't you be consistent?

ILD: Try to be consistent.

The others nod in somber agreement.

CHIP: I can tell you what the graffiti said. I can tell you about the worn-out tape recorder. I can tell you about Runciter's television commercial, the note in the carton of cigarettes in Baltimore—I can tell you about the label on the flask of Elixir of Ubique. But I can't make it all add up. In any case, we have to get to your hotel to try to reach Edie Dorn before she withers away and irreversibly expires. Where can we get a taxi?

DON DENNY: The mortuary has provided us with two cars to use while we're here. Those Pierce-Arrows sitting over there; no extra charge.

Another "Andy Warhol" spraycan manifestation. The label reads:

WE WANTED TO GIVE YOU A SHAVE LIKE NO OTHER YOU EVER HAD. WE SAID, IT'S ABOUT TIME A MAN'S FACE GOT A LITTLE LOVING. WE SAID, WITH UBIK'S SELF-WINDING SWISS CHROMIUM NEVER ENDING BLADE, THE DAYS OF SCRAPE SCRAPE ARE OVER. SO TRY UBIK. AND BE LOVED. WARNING: USE ONLY AS DIRECTED. AND WITH CAUTION.

When the spraycan manifestation fades away we see:

34.

The two identical Pierce-Arrow sedans moving majestically through Des Moines 1930's traffic. Then pan up to JOE CHIP *seated with others of the group,* DON DENNY *beside him.* CHIP *appears deep in gloomy introspection; obviously he is acutely worried, and wishes the cars would move faster, although he is the driver; all moves slowly.*

CHIP: (*Filter*) There is something wrong with my theory. Edie Dorn, by being with the group, should have been immune. And I—it should have been me who began to die. Sometime during that long slow airflight from New York. (CHIP *turns to* DON DENNY, *speaks aloud.*)

What we'll have to do is make certain that anyone who feels tired—that seems to be the first warning—tells the rest of us. Immediately. And isn't allowed to wander away.

DON DENNY: Do you all hear that? As soon as any of you feels tired, even a little bit, report it to either Mister Chip or myself. (DON DENNY *lowers his voice, speaks to* CHIP.) And then what?

PAT: And then what, Joe. Tell us what to do then. We're listening.

CHIP: It seems strange to me that your talent isn't coming into play. This situation appears to me to be made for it. Why can't you go back fifteen minutes and compel Edie Dorn not to wander off? Do what you did when G.G. Ashwood first introduced us.

WE WANTED TO GIVE YOU A SHAVE LIKE NO OTHER YOU EVER HAD. WE SAID, IT'S ABOUT TIME A MAN'S FACE GOT A LITTLE LOVING. WE SAID, WITH UBIK'S SELF-WINDING SWISS CHROMIUM NEVER ENDING BLADE, THE DAYS OF SCRAPE SCRAPE ARE OVER. SO TRY UBIK. AND BE LOVED. WARNING: USE ONLY AS DIRECTED. AND WITH CAUTION.

UBIK: The Screenplay

PAT: That was just an interior trip I put you on; it wasn't real.

CHIP: I don't believe that. My trip was real. I almost made it into that coin shop.

DON DENNY: It's hard to tell what's real, now.

CHIP: I'll tell you what's real. Everything is real. Did you think of that? (CHIP *studies* PAT *acutely.*) So you're not going to do anything.

ILD: They had a fight last night while we were eating dinner. Miss Conley and Miss Dorn. Miss Conley doesn't like her; that's why she won't help.

PAT: I liked Edie.

DON DENNY: Do you have any reason for not making use of your talent? Joe's right; it's very strange and difficult to understand —at least for me—why exactly you don't try to help.

PAT: My talent doesn't work any more. It hasn't since the bomb blast on Luna.

CHIP: Why didn't you say so?

PAT: Why should I volunteer information like that, and get fired right away, after just being hired? I keep trying and it keeps not working; nothing happens. And its never been that way before. I've had the talent virtually my entire life. Maybe it's because we're back in this archaic barbaric old time period; maybe psionic talents don't work in 1939. But that wouldn't explain Luna—unless we had already traveled back here and we didn't realize it. (PAT *lapses into brooding, introverted silence, a bitter expression on her usually wild face.*)

Maybe we're outside of time. (*Glancing at* CHIP *intently.*)

Of course a time-traveling talent would no longer function if we're outside of time, if this isn't really 1939. If say this is—half-life.

CHIP: You know, things can happen to you so much worse than you ever anticipated. Worse that your worst anxieties. The universe can think up far worse things that your own mind.

ILD: Like, the worst fear I ever had up to now was that—you'll laugh. That when I flushed the toilet, the handle would fall off.

CHIP: (CHIP *and the others laugh.*) Symbolism.

111

Philip K. Dick

ILD: (*Flushing angrily*) Come on, now. Cut it out.

CHIP: Do I keep going straight here?

TIPPY JACKSON: Turn right.

PAT: You'll see a brick building with a neon sign going up and down. Or maybe it's a lot of separate incandescent bulbs; who knows? The Meremont Hotel, it's called. A terrible place. One bathroom for every two rooms, and a tub instead of a shower. And the food; incredible. And the only drink they sell is something called Nehi.

DON DENNY: I like the food. Genuine meat of the cow, rather than protein synthetics. Authentic salmon, no preservatives; you'd suppose the people here would life forever.

ILD: They would, if their medical knowledge was as advanced as ours. With their diet and our medical knowledge together ...

CHIP: Is your money good? (CHIP *has speeded the car up; now we—and he—hear a high pitched far off echoing siren, coming nearer.*) What the hell's that mean?

DON DENNY: I don't know.

They all are confused and nervous.

SAMMY MUNDO: It's a police siren. You were speeding and you didn't give a hand signal before you turned. I've been watching the other cars; that's what they do, the driver sticks his hand out.

Siren is very close and loud, now. CHIP *pulls over to the curb and parks. Giant cop gets off 1930's style police motorcycle, strolls over, leans in to peer at* CHIP *and the others.*

COP: Let me see your license, mister.

CHIP: I don't have one. Just make out the ticket and let us go. We're on our way back from a funeral.

COP: At the speed you were driving—

CHIP: I know. "We were on our way *to* a funeral." Just write out the ticket.

COP: Let's see your identification. (CHIP *passes the* COP *his wallet;* COP *writes out citation, has* CHIP *sign it, then tears it off and hands it to* CHIP.)

Failure to signal. Unsafe speed. No operator's license. The

UBIK: The Screenplay

citation tells where and when to appear.

CHIP: I have to *appear*? It isn't a fine I can mail in?

COP: I can take you in with me now, if that'll be easier on you.

CHIP: How much is this going to cost me?

CHIP *examines the citation; the* COP, *meanwhile, saunters off and remounts his motorcycle; he roars off. We see a close up of the citation; it's the same handwriting we saw on the men's room wall, and it reads:* YOU ARE IN MUCH GREATER DANGER THAN I THOUGHT. WHAT PAT CONLEY SAID IS—

There the handwritten message breaks off. CHIP *turns the citation over, finds nothing on the back, no continuation. While he is wondering about this,* ILD *takes the citation and examines it.*

ILD: Wow, this is unusual. You must have had some identification of Pat's in your wallet. The officer must mean there's a defect in the car that he observed, a safety hazard. (ILD *studies further as* CHIP *starts the car moving away from the curb. Reading aloud from the citation* ILD *continues:*)

"Try Archer's Drugstore for reliable household remedies and medicinal—" (CHIP *buckingly halts the car again; he turns, glares at* ILD, *who slinks down in his set uneasily.*)

It's an ad, Mister Chip. At the bottom of the citation. In squirrel agate type.

CHIP: (*Exasperation*) Finish reading it.

ILD: "—medicinal preparations of tried and tested value. Economically priced." That's it. (ILD *hands citation back to* CHIP, *who continues to glare at him.*) Don't be sore at me, Mister Chip; I didn't put it there.

PAT: Could we get started, or have you forgotten about Edie Dorn?

Getting out of the car, CHIP *walks across sidewalk to the nearest store, a magazine-candy-and-tobacco place; he approaches proprietor.*

CHIP: Can I use your phonebook?

PROPRIETOR: In the rear.

In the rear of the shop, CHIP *searches through phonebook; we see comic books of the late 1930's:* Tip Top, King Comics, Popular Comics. *Kids can be seen reading them. There are also big jars of* candy, as well as candy behind the glass counters. Having had no luck with the phonebook, CHIP *returns to counter, where* PROPRIETOR *is selling two rolls of Necco wafers to a kid.*

CHIP: Do you know by any chance where I can find Archer's Drugstore?

PROPRIETOR: Nowhere. At least, not any more.

CHIP: Why not?

PROPRIETOR: It's been closed for years.

CHIP: Tell me where it was anyhow. Draw me a map.

PROPRIETOR: You don't need a map; I can point to where it was. You see that barber pole there? Go over to that side of the street and then look north. You'll see an old false-front building with gables, yellow in color. There's a couple of apartments over there still in use, but the store premises downstairs, they're abandoned; you'll be able to make out the sign, though: Archer's Drugs. What happened to Ed Archer was his cancer . . . (*Fade out*)

Dissolve.

35.

We see JOE CHIP *standing before Archer's Drugs. It appears to be the same drugstore which kept going by again and again during his trip with* BLISS *in the Willys-Knight. But there is something even more odd about it, which obviously baffles* CHIP, *too. The old building seems to oscillate at regular intervals into something else which shimmers and is insubstantial. This other state, we see, consists of a retail store from the future: from 1992,* JOE CHIP's *original actual time. It is enormous and complex, somewhat like the supermarket which we saw in the Baltimore scene; it is obviously past our own time, whereas Archer's Drugs is from our past.* CHIP *poises himself as the two alternate time-period entities come and go, and then, when Archer's Drugs is in phase, he moves swiftly forward, entering its old-fashioned rococo doorway.*

36.

Interior of Archer's Drugstore. It is not abandoned. We and CHIP *see hernia belts, rows of corrective eyeglasses, a sign reading* LEECHES, *a mortar and pestle, huge glass-stoppered bottles that contain old-time medicines; everything is dark in color, somber: much like the interior of the Simple Shepherd Mortuary. Wall clock has Latin numerals, and a pendulum; only sound we hear is its ticking.* CHIP *discovers a little round bell on counter; presses the ringer. From behind heavy velvet drapes in the rear, a wispy young man wearing a gray suit with vest, appears; he is the druggist.*

DRUGGIST: Yes sir?

CHIP: I'd like a jar of Ubik.

DRUGGIST: The salve?

Strangely, the DRUGGIST*'s lip-synch is out;* CHIP *sees this, as do we, so it's evidently not a film failure. The* DRUGGIST*'s words are heard first; then his lips move.*

CHIP: Is it a salve? I thought it was for internal use.

Weirdly, the DRUGGIST *does not respond; it's as if some gulf exists between them, an epoch of time.* CHIP *can see* DRUGGIST, *and* DRUGGIST *evidently sees him, but they are not in the same world together, as if the* DRUGGIST *is guessing at what* CHIP *says, perhaps, rather than actually hearing it. Then finally the* DRUGGIST*'s mouth opens again; his lips move. Presently, still out of synch, words are audible.*

DRUGGIST: Ubik has undergone many permutations as the manufacturer has improved it. You may be familiar with the old Ubik, rather than the new.

The DRUGGIST *turns to one side, but his movement has a stop-action quality; even as he moves it's as if slowed (i.e. in film sequences where camera is run at higher speed than projection speed). The subjective impression we get in watching him is that he appears to be moving in a liquid medium—perhaps a denser atmosphere on some other, heavier planet: not our own. He does* not *bound dream-like, weightless; on the contrary.*

DRUGGIST: We have had a great deal of difficulty obtaining Ubik of late.

Now the DRUGGIST *returns to counter, walking as if through Jello; he carries a flat leaded tin which he places before* CHIP *on the prescription counter. Astoundingly, the tin is misplaced by the* DRUGGIST *slightly above the counter, but it at once sinks down to come to rest, as if hydraulically lowered.* CHIP *watches in stunned perplexity.*

Philip K. Dick

DRUGGIST: This comes in the form of a powder to which you add coal tar. The Ubik powder, however, is dear. Forty dollars.

CHIP: What's in it?

The high price has obviously chilled him.

DRUGGIST: That is the manufacturer's secret.

CHIP *picks up the sealed tin and holds it to light source.*

CHIP: Is it all right if I read the label?

DRUGGIST: Of course.

It's necessary for CHIP *to carry the leaded tin out to front of store to capture light from street. Writing on label is same holography as traffic citation; it reads: ABSOLUTELY UNTRUE. SHE DID NOT—REPEAT, NOT—TRY TO USE HER TALENT FOLLOWING THE BOMB BLAST. SHE DID NOT TRY TO RESTORE WENDY WRIGHT OR AL HAMMOND OR EDI DORN. SHE'S LYING TO YOU, JOE, AND THAT MAKES ME RETHINK THE WHOLE SITUATION. I'LL LET YOU KNOW AS SOON AS I COME TO A CONCLUSION. MEANWHILE, BE VERY CAREFUL. BY THE WAY: UBIK POWDER IS OF UNIVERSAL HEALING VALUE IF DIRECTIONS FOR USE ARE RIGOROUSLY AND CONSCIENTIOUSLY FOLLOWED.*

CHIP: (*Returns to where* DRUGGIST *stands watching.*) Can I make you out a check?

DRUGGIST: (*The* DRUGGIST's *lips move; no sound.*)

CHIP: Pardon?

DRUGGIST: (*Lips do not move*) You're not from Des Moines. I can tell by your accent. No, I'd have to know you to take a check that large.

CHIP: Credit card, then?

DRUGGIST: Could you speak more clearly? Can't quite make out—

Setting down the tin of Ubik, CHIP *leaves drugstore. Camera follows him across street, where he pauses, looks back. We see, from where he just came, what he sees: only a vacant, dilapidated yellow building, tatters of curtains in its upstairs windows, the ground floor boarded up and deserted! Through the spaces between the boards we see only gaping darkness, the cavity of broken windows, without life.*

CHIP: (*Filter*) So that's it—the opportunity to buy a tin of Ubik

UBIK: The Screenplay

powder is gone. Even if I were to find forty dollars lying on the pavement in front of me. But I did get hold of the rest of Runciter's warning. For what that's worth. But it may not even be true. It may be only a misguided opinion by a dying brain— or by a totally dead brain—as in the case of the TV commercial.

Slowly, CHIP *moves off along sidewalk. Other persons have stopped walking here and there; they stare up at the sky.* CHIP, *absorbed in gloom, does not look up, but we see what they see: an old biplane, skywriting. Its smoke message:* KEEP THE OLD SWIZER UP, JOE!

37.

Lobby of the Meremont Hotel: high-ceilinged, provincial, crimson-carpeted, deteriorated, ugly chandelier with many yellow bulbs, on now, during daytime. Soundtrack at high level: the "Gloria" from Beethoven's "Missa Solemnis." In the music much motion; in the lobby none. CHIP *and* DON DENNY *sit in overstuffed easychairs, with sand-type floor ashtrays on each side of them. Music continues as if* CHIP *and* DON DENNY *are themselves hearing it; they gaze dully forward; abruptly, music shuts off;* CHIP *and* DON DENNY *stir about, as if in a concert intermission.*

DON DENNY: We found her.

CHIP: Edie, you mean.

DON DENNY: It's all over—for her, anyhow. And it wasn't attractive. Now Fred Zafsky is gone. I thought he was in the other car, and they thought he went along with us. Apparently, he didn't get into either car. He must be back at the mortuary.

CHIP: (*Getting out a little pouch of tobacco and papers; rolls a cigarette.*) It's happening faster now. (CHIP's *hands shake too much; he can't even lift the paper to his lips to lick it.*) Can we get a drink here? What about money? Mine's worthless.

DON DENNY: The mortuary is paying for everything. Runciter's instructions to them.

CHIP: The hotel tab, too? How the hell was that arranged? (*Gets out the citation the* COP *wrote him, hands it to* DON DENNY.) I want you to look at this citation. While no one else is with us. I have the rest of the message; that's where I've been—getting it.

DON DENNY: (*Studies citation; his face becomes stern.*) Runciter thinks Pat Conley is lying. You realize what that would mean? It means she could have nullified all this. Everything that's happened to us, starting with Runciter's death.

CHIP: It could mean more than that.

DENNY *uncorks metal tube, slides expensive cigar from it; he bites off end of cigar, spitting end into the sand-type ashtray. Very slowly and expertly he lights up the big cigar.*

DON DENNY: You're right. You're absolutely right.

CHIP: (*Again trying—and failing—to roll cigarette.*) I don't particularly like to think about it. I don't like anything about it. It's worse. A lot worse than what I thought before.

DON DENNY: Try one of these.

DON DENNY *passes cigar tube to* CHIP. *Uncorking it,* CHIP *like* DENNY *bites off cigar-end expertly and so forth; they now sit together smoking identical cigars, in a leisurely way, as if they've been doing this all their adult lives.*

DON DENNY: What do you think of it?

CHIP: Very good.

DON DENNY: All Havana filler.

CHIP: This is a lot more serious than I thought before, what Al Hammond believed, for example. Which was bad enough.

DON DENNY: But this could be it.

CHIP: Throughout all that's been happening I've kept trying to understand why. I was sure if I knew why—

DON DENNY: (*Warningly*) Don't say anything to the rest of them. This may not be true, and even if it is, knowing it isn't going to help them.

PAT CONLEY: Knowing what?

Unexpectedly, PAT *appears from out of their view and our view; she is present abruptly, and her smoldering, intense personality at once intimidates the two seated men; they pause, cigars half-raised to their lips.*

PAT CONLEY: It's a shame about Edie Dorn. And Fred Zafsky; I suppose he is gone, too. That doesn't really leave very many of us, does it? I wonder who'll be next? (PAT *nonchalantly seats herself on the arm of* CHIP*'s chair, far too close to him for his comfort.*) Tippy is lying down in her room. She didn't say she felt tired, but I think we must assume she is. Don't you agree?

UBIK: The Screenplay

DON DENNY: Yes, I agree.

Both men carefully keep their eyes fixed on PAT, *warily.*

PAT: How did you make out with your citation, Joe?

PAT *relentlessly holds out her hand, authority-figure-wise.*

PAT: Can I look at it?

CHIP *pauses a moment. Then wordlessly extends the folded citation toward her.* DON DENNY, *watching, stiffly resumes smoking.*

PAT: How did the policeman know my name? Why is there something here about me?

DON DENNY: (*In an aside—stage-whisper, old-time style—to* CHIP.) She doesn't recognize his writing. Because she was just hired.

CHIP: You're doing it, aren't you Pat? It's you and your talent. We're here in this place because of you.

DON DENNY: (DON DENNY *smiles to himself, twitches as he speaks.*) And you're killing us off. One by one. But why? (*To* CHIP) What reason could she have? She doesn't even know us, not really.

CHIP: (*To* PAT) Is this why you came to Runciter Associates? G.G. Ashwood scouted you and brought you in. Was he working for Ray Hollis, is that it? Is that what really happened to us—*not the bomb blast but you?*

PAT's *black, enormous eyes expand in response. The lobby of the hotel blows up, as if totally detonated—shredded into fragments which churn forward in a swirl. Mixed with the bits of the hotel are bits of words: pieces of the previous spraycan label messages. We see these molecules of the "manifestations" intermixed with molecules of the hotel lobby, catching sight of the key word UBIK now and then, more so than any other single word, but these are all words and word-fragments we've seen before; nothing new to us. Behind all this storm of exploded particles we catch the dim outline of a huge "Andy Warhol" spraycan that seems to be attempting but failing to manifest itself; it fades out again, and then total black-out.*

Philip K. Dick

38.

On the screen: still blackness. Audio track:

YOUNG WOMAN'S VOICE: Lift your arms and be all at once curvier! New extra-gentle Ubik bra and longline Ubik special bra mean, lift your arms and be all at once curvier!

On screen, fade in: lovely female mid-section, like Aphrodite herself: totally nude, with extraordinarily perfect bare breasts, in best possible lighting.

YOUNG WOMAN'S VOICE: Yes, lift your arms and be all at once curvier!

Girl on screen lifts her arms; it is as promised. Breasts project in wonderfully classical way, to the joy of all of us.

YOUNG WOMAN'S VOICE: Supplies firm, relaxing support to bosom all day long, when fitted as directed.

On screen mid-torso pose remains; there is no bra even yet. None is needed. None will ever be needed. Sound-track silent, now; we see the single word UBIK pass slowly left to right across female torso and disappear. End of "manifestation."

39.

Visual flickering; like with hand-cranked projector. Again the lobby of the Meremont Hotel, but very dim, as if "bulb" is weak in "projector." Colors washed out, low hues only; yellow filter over everything. We see DON DENNY *and* JOE CHIP *standing together;* DON DENNY *is supporting* JOE CHIP *who appears weak and drooping, as if unable to stand alone.*

DON DENNY: What's the matter, Joe? What's wrong?

CHIP: I'm okay. I just feel tired.

CHIP *shakes his head, to clear it. He is confused.*

DON DENNY: Let me help you to a chair.

CHIP: I'm okay! Just let me sit down.

DON DENNY: (*To* PAT) What did you do to him?

CHIP: She didn't do anything to me.

The spacial relationships of the lobby alter; it becomes ominously large, the sound echoing; we see it as CHIP *sees it, with the furniture and people far-off. His own voice has an unnatural squeaky sound.*

CHIP: I want to go upstairs and lie down.

We hear now a constant tone; about 8 kHz; it obscures all other sounds somewhat.

DON DENNY: I'll get you a room. (*Colors in the lobby ebb to dull red, smoky as well.*) You stay in that chair, Joe; I'll be right back.

Vague shape of DON DENNY *retreating.*

PAT: Anything I can do for you?

CHIP: No. A cigarette maybe. Do you have one?

PAT: (*Pleasantly*) Sorry. No got.

CHIP: What's the matter with me?

PAT: Cardiac arrest, maybe.

CHIP: Do you think there's a hotel doctor?

PAT: I doubt it.

CHIP: You won't see? You won't look?

PAT: I think it's merely psychosomatic. You're not really sick. You'll recover.

DON DENNY: (*Returning*) I've got a room for you, Joe. On the second floor; room 203. So you won't have to go very far up to get there. Joe, you look awful. Frail—like you're about to blow away. My God, Joe, do you know what you look like? You look like Edie Dorn looked when we found her.

PAT: Oh, nothing like that. Edie Dorn is dead. Joe isn't dead; are you, Joe?

CHIP: I want to go upstairs. I want to lie down. (CHIP *gets to his feet; lobby tilts. Shapes loom and recede.*) Where's the elevator?

DON DENNY: I'll lead you over to it. You're like a feather. What's happening to you, Joe? Can you say? Do you know? Try to tell me.

PAT: He doesn't know.

DON DENNY: I think he should have a doctor. Right away.

CHIP: No.

Philip K. Dick

DON DENNY: I'll go get a doctor. Pat, you stay here with him; don't let him out of your sight! I'll be back as soon as I can.

Vague sight of DON DENNY's *form retreating, then entirely gone.*

PAT: Well, Joe, what do you want? What can I do for you? Just name it.

CHIP: The elevator.

PAT: You want me to lead you over to the elevator? I'll be glad to.

CHIP: Not so fast.

CHIP *has terrible trouble walking. Shapes come and go, as if he is at the bottom of the ocean and they are all strange life forms.*

CHIP: Just get me into the elevator.

Now we and CHIP *can discern the elevator. Several persons stand waiting for it. Old-fashioned dial above, with baroque needle.*

PAT: It'll be along in a sec.

From her purse she gets cigarettes, lights up—what she told him before about a cigarette evidently wasn't true.

PAT: It's a very ancient kind of elevator. You know what I think? I think it's one of those old open iron cages. Do they scare you?

Elevator needle passes two, reaches one. Doors slide aside. We and CHIP *see the grill of the open cage, the metal latticework. The uniformed attendant seated on a stool, his hand on the rotating control.*

ELEVATOR OPERATOR: Going up. Move to the back, please.

CHIP: I'm not going up in that.

It is the same old open-cage elevator CHIP *"hallucinated" before.*

PAT: Why not? Do you think the cable will break? Is that what terrifies you? I can see you're terrified. Well, Joe Chip; the only other way to your room is the stairs. And you aren't going to be able to climb the stairs, not in your condition.

CHIP: (*With last burst of anger toward her.*) What is my condition?

PAT: Pretty close to—well, let's say, not too good a condition.

CHIP: I'll go up by the stairs.

By himself, CHIP *moves away from elevator. However, he becomes lost in swirling vague forms almost at once: disoriented.*

PAT: There we are. Right in front of you. Just take hold of the railing and go bump-de-bump upstairs to bed. See?

Momentary clear vision of PAT *scrambling up stairs lithely, with no difficulty or effort.*

PAT: Can you make it?

CHIP: I—don't—want you. To come—with—me.

PAT: Oh dear. Are you afraid I'll take advantage of your condition? Do something to you, something harmful or, you know, nasty?

CHIP: No. I just want to be by myself. So I can—think—and figure it out.

Now CHIP *begins his painful, labored ascent of the stairs.*

PAT: Mister Denny asked me to stay with you. I can read to you or get you things. I can wait on you.

CHIP: (*Gasping*) Alone!

PAT: May I watch you climb? I'd like to see how long it takes you. Assuming you make it at all.

CHIP: I'll make it.

PAT: I wonder if this is what Wendy did. She was the first; right?

CHIP: I was . . . in love with . . . her.

PAT: Oh, I know. G.G. Ashwood told me. He read your mind. G.G. and I got to be very good friends; we spent a lot of time together. You might say we had a ball. Yes, you could say that.

CHIP: My theory . . . our theory . . . was right. The one . . . that you and G.G. worked it out with Ray Hollis. To infiltrate.

PAT: Quite right.

She is continually visible above him on the stairs, but offering him no help, her eyes fixed on him; she is smiling.

CHIP: Our best inertials. And Runciter! Wipe us all out at once. We're not in half-life; we're not—

PAT: Oh you can *die*. You're not dead—not you, Joe Chip, in particular, I mean. But frankly speaking, you are dying off one by one. But why jabber on and on about it? Why keep rehashing it? You said it all a little while ago, and frankly, you bore me, going over it again and again. You're really a very dull, pedantic person, Joe Chip. Almost as dull as Wendy Wright.

You two would have made a good pair.

CHIP: That's why Wendy died first. Not because she had separated from the group, but because—

Unable to climb at all, and barely able to speak, CHIP *stands hanging on to the rail, attempting to get his breath. We and he see his arm and hand extended to the metal rail; his arm and hand have a weak, thin, trembling look: that of advanced old age. With his other hand,* CHIP *reaches fumblingly, takes hold of his sleeve—the fabric tears readily. Dried, starved material, parting like cheap paper; it has no strength in its fibers. It is the color of a paperwasps' nest: a gray. Looking back down the stairs,* CHIP *sees a trail of what appears to be crumbled cloth fragments. Left behind by him.*

PAT: Feel any better?

CHIP: I'm going to make it.

PAT: Maybe so; it's not much further.

CHIP: Farther.

PAT: You're incredible. So trivial, so small! Even in your own death spasms you—or I mean what probably seems subjectively to you as death spasms. I shouldn't have used that term, "death spasms."

PAT *is talking fast; she has made a mistake.*

CHIP: No, you shouldn't have.

PAT: No, it might depress you. Try to be optimistic, okay?

CHIP: (*More firmly now*) Just tell me how many steps. Left.

PAT: Six. No sorry; ten. Or is it nine? I think it's nine. In fact you're almost there. (PAT *stares brightly at him as he again laboriously, slowly ascends.*) What do you have to say, Joe Chip? Any immortal comments on your great climb? The greatest climb in the history of man. No, that's not true. Wendy and Al and Edie and Fred Zafsky did it before you. But this is the only one I've actually gotten to watch.

CHIP: Why me?

PAT: I *want* to watch you, Joe Chip, because of your low-class little scheme back in Zurich. Of having Wendy Wright spend the night with you in your trashy-modern hotel room. Now tonight, here, it will be different. You'll be alone.

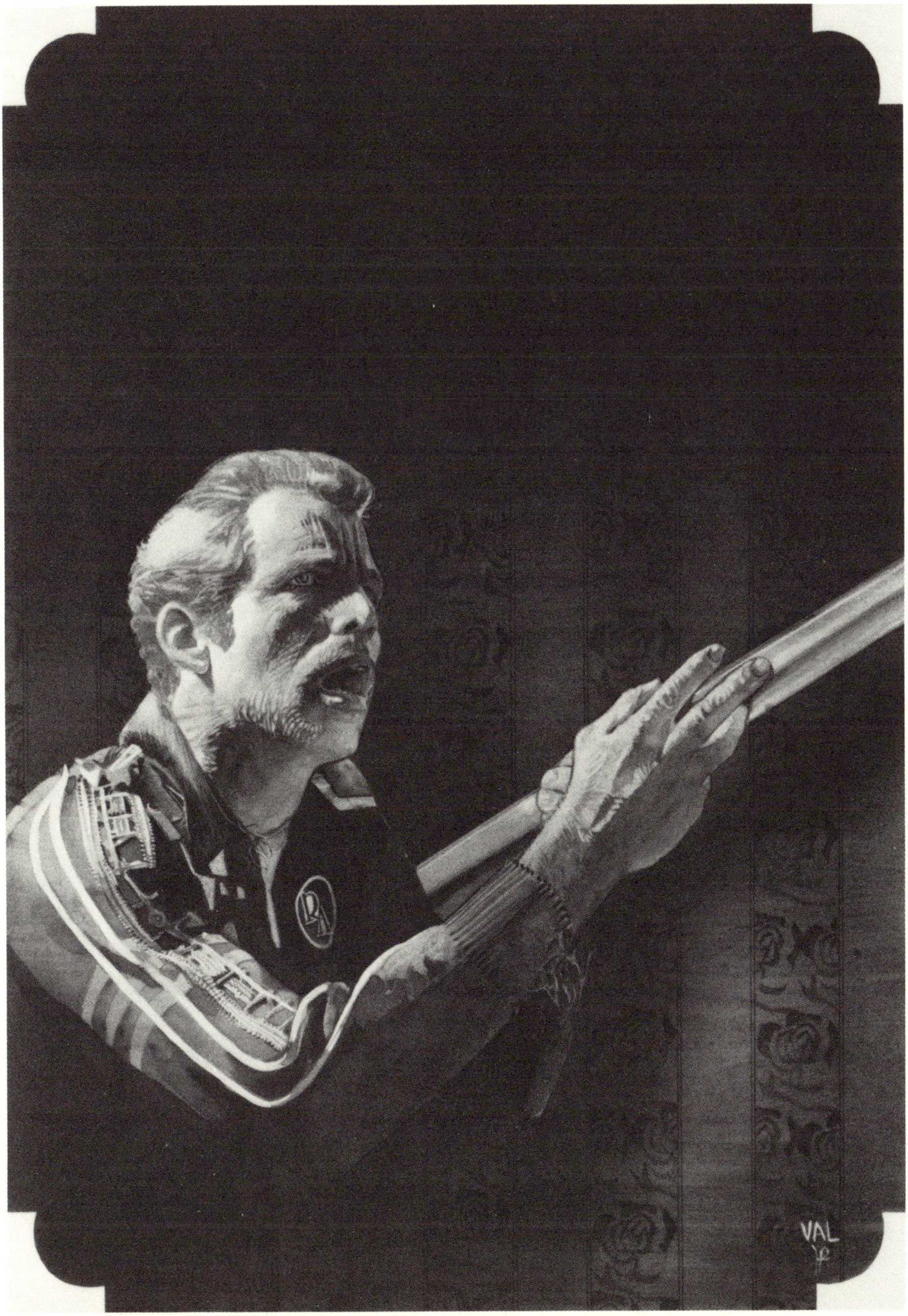
VAL

CHIP: That night, too. I was alone.

He halts as he sees above him drifts of snow on the stairs: not deep but more a frosting-over, due to a decline in temperature. Still, the sparkling silvery texture is there; and, as PAT above him breathes, we can see the pale cloud of her exhalation adding to the impression of cold: as if it, somehow, is emanating from within her.

PAT: Do you have your key?

When she speaks, now, more frost is exhaled over everything, and directly at CHIP: as if they're within a small confined area, such as one experiences in a car or a small freezer-locker.

CHIP: Key.

PAT: Room key. Key to your hotel room. Think how awful you'd feel if you arrived at last on the second floor only to find you had lost your key and couldn't get into your room.

CHIP: I have it. (*Steadies himself, searches pockets for his key.*) It's here.

His coat rips away, in mere shreds now; the pieces fall from him, and from a top pocket, the key slides out. Key falls two steps down, below him. Beyond his reach.

PAT: I'll get it for you.

She darts agilely by him, scoops up key; she holds the key to the light to examine it, then carries it briskly to the top of the stairs and sets it down on railing.

PAT: Right up here. Where you can reach it when you're all through climbing. Your reward. The room, I believe, is to the left, about four doors down the hall. You'll have to move slowly, but it'll be a lot easier once you're off the stairs. Once you don't have to climb against gravity.

CHIP: I can see the key. And the top. I can see the top of the stairs.

Watching him, PAT offers no assistance as CHIP at last manages to haul himself to level ground: the wooden door marked SECOND FLOOR.

PAT: Goodbye, Joe. You don't want Don Denny bursting in, do you? A doctor won't be able to help you anyhow; so I'll tell him I got the hotel people to call a cab and that you're on your way across town to a hospital. That way you won't be bothered.

UBIK: The Screenplay

You can lie in your room entirely by yourself and no one will knock or give you any trouble. Is that what you want?

CHIP: (*Panting in exhaustion*) Yes.

PAT: Okay, then here is the key. Keep your chin up, as they say here in 1939. Don't take any wooden nickels. They say that, too; all the time. What time there is anyhow, left. Have a good time, Joe Chip. Have a good nap. Go to sleep, Joe, and get some rest.

As CHIP *opens SECOND FLOOR door,* PAT *dwindles and is gone from his and our sight. Now he is alone. Gripping the key he balances himself against the open door, then starts step by step down the corridor, supporting himself by means of the fly-specked wall. We are given a sense of him colliding with vague shapes, but his nebulous view is ours, too; we see only dimly a numbered door go past, then the kinetic sense of falling, of him picking himself up and still going on, perhaps on hands and knees, now, perhaps crawling. But at last he is at the right door; again erect, he is searching for key hole. We see close up of key missing, then finally entering lock. Again, the impression we get is one of* CHIP *trembling from cold rather than from fatigue alone. Sound of door opening, bumping; noise of* CHIP *stumbling into the hotel room. We see dusty carpet, tall window with tied-back dingy-white lace curtains. Brass bed now wheels into view;* CHIP *is making his way toward it. Key falls to floor as he progresses. We sense him reaching yearningly for the bed, to lie down there, to rest—*

And then we see a figure seated in an overstuffed easy chair, facing him. The hotel room at once locks into focus. The cobwebs (e.g. fisheye lens et al) are gone. It is GLEN RUNCITER *sitting there, saying nothing, simply watching* JOE CHIP. RUNCITER *is dressed as we saw him last; he is unchanged.*

RUNCITER: I couldn't help you climb the damn stairs; she would have seen me. Matter of fact, I was afraid she'd come all the way into the room here, along with you, to torment you right to the end. We'd have been in trouble, because she—

Suddenly RUNCITER *is on his feet; he assists* CHIP—*not to the bed—but to a straight-backed wooden chair.*

RUNCITER: We'll talk about that later. Here. Can you hold on a few seconds longer? I want to shut and lock the door. In case she changes her mind.

In three big steps RUNCITER *reaches the door, slams it, bolts it, returns to* CHIP, *scrutinizes him, then crosses to a wooden vanity*

Philip K. Dick

table; RUNCITER *opens drawer, hastily brings out a spray can with bright stripes, balloons and lettering glorifying its shiny surfaces.*

RUNCITER: Ubik.

RUNCITER *shakes the spraycan mightily, then stands directly before* CHIP, *aiming it at him.*

RUNCITER: Don't thank me for this.

With expert aim, RUNCITER *sprays prolongedly left and right; the air in the hotel room visibly flickers with mica-like shiny particles in suspension: it shimmers as if bright elements of light have been released, as if the sun's energy has suddenly entered this worn-out elderly hotel room.*

RUNCITER: Feel better? It should work on you right away. You should already be getting a positive reaction.

CHIP: Do you have a cigarette?

RUNCITER: No filter tips; they don't have filtration devices on their cigarettes in this backward, no-good time-period. (RUNCITER *extends pack of Camels toward* CHIP.) I'll light it for you.

RUNCITER *extends match, which he ignites with his thumb-nail.*

CHIP: It's fresh—the cigarette.

RUNCITER: Oh hell yes. Christ, I just now bought it downstairs at the tobacco counter. You know they've got packs of cigarettes for ten cents? The premium brands are fifteen. Oh yeah; we're a long way into this—well past the stage of clotted milk and stale cigarettes that crumble away.

CHIP: "Into" this?

RUNCITER: Yeah, "into," not "out of." There's a difference.

Lights cigarette for himself, too.

CHIP: Can you help the rest of the group?

RUNCITER: I have exactly one can of this Ubik. Most of it I had to use on you. Joe, my ability to alter conditions here is limited. I've done what I could; I got through to you—all of you—every chance I got. Hell, you missed two-thirds of my intrusions to you—they went unnoticed. I used every way I could, every method. I did everything I had the capacity to bring about—

we're talking about something extremely difficult. And extremely dense as well. No offense meant; it has been discouraging to me, too. So little communication—so much work, so little achieved. Almost nothing.

CHIP: The graffiti on the bathroom walls. You wrote that we were dead and you were alive.

RUNCITER: I *am* alive. Contrary to some reports.

CHIP: Are we dead, the rest of us?

RUNCITER: (*Pauses*) Yes.

CHIP: But in the taped TV commercial—

RUNCITER: Goddam it, Joe, that was for the purpose of getting you to *fight*! To find Ubik! It made you look and you kept on looking too. I kept trying and trying to get it to you, but you know what went wrong; she kept drawing everything into the past—she worked on us all with that talent of hers. Over and over again she regressed it and made it—Ubik itself—worthless. Except for the fragmentary notes, the words here and there I managed to slip to you in conjunction with the stuff. Look what I've been up against—the same thing that got all of you, that's killed you off one by one. Frankly, it's amazing to me that I was able to do as much as I did.

CHIP: When did you figure out what was taking place? Did you always know? From the start?

RUNCITER: "The start." What's that mean? It started months ago or maybe even years ago; God knows how long Hollis and Mick and Pat Conley and S. Dole Melipone and G.G. Ashwood have been hatching it up, working it over and reworking it like dough. Here's what happened. We got lured to Luna. We let Pat Conley come with us, a person we didn't know, a talent we didn't understand—which possibly even Hollis doesn't understand. An ability anyhow connected with time reversions; not, strictly speaking, the ability to travel through time—for instance, she can't go into the future. In a certain sense, she can't go into the past either; what she does, as near as I can comprehend it, is start a counter-process that uncovers the prior stages inherent in configurations of matter. But you know that; you and Al Hammond figured it out. Al Hammond—what a loss. But I couldn't do anything; I couldn't break through then as I've done now.

CHIP: Why were you able to now?

RUNCITER: Because this is as far back as she is able to carry us. Normal forward flow has already resumed; we're again flowing from past into present into future. She evidently stretched her ability to its limit. 1939; that's the limit. What she's done now is shut off her talent. Why not? She's accomplished what Ray Hollis sent her to us to do.

CHIP: How many people have been affected? The whole world?

RUNCITER: No, just the group of us who were on Luna there in that dome. Not even Zoe Wirt. Pat can circumscribe the range of the field she creates. As far as the rest of the world is concerned, the bunch of us took off for Luna and got blown up in an accidental explosion; we were put into cold-pac by solicitous Stanton Mick, but no contact could be established—they "didn't get us soon enough."

CHIP: Why wouldn't the bomb blast be enough? (*Raising an eyebrow,* RUNCITER *eyes him without answering.*) Why use Pat Conley at all? There's no reason for all this reversion machinery, this sinking us into a retrograde time momentum back here to 1939. It serves no purpose.

RUNCITER: That's an interesting point. I'll have to think about it. Give me a little while.

RUNCITER *walks to window, stands gazing out.*

CHIP: It strikes me that what we appear to be faced with is a malignant force, rather than a purposeful force. Not so much someone trying to kill us or nullify us, someone trying to eliminate us from functioning as a prudence organization, but—hell, Glen—an irresponsible entity that's enjoying what it's doing to us! The way it's killing us off one by one—it doesn't have to prolong all this. That doesn't sound to me like Ray Hollis; he deals in cold, practical murder at worst. And from what I know about Stanton Mick—

RUNCITER: Pat Conley herself. She's psychologically a sadistic person. Like tearing wings off flies. Playing with us.

CHIP: It sounds to me more like a child.

RUNCITER: But look at Pat; she's spiteful and jealous. She got Wendy first because of emotional animosity. She followed you all the way up the stairs just now, gloating over it, in fact.

UBIK: The Screenplay

CHIP: How do you know that? You were in this room. Also—

RUNCITER: (*Raggedly*) I haven't told you all of it. As a matter of fact, what I've been saying isn't strictly true. I don't hold the same relationship to this regressed world that the rest of you do; you're absolutely right. I know too much. It's because I enter it from outside, Joe.

CHIP: Manifestations.

RUNCITER: Yes. Thrust down into this world, here and there. At strategic points and times. Like the traffic citation. Like Archer's.

CHIP: You didn't tape that commercial. That was live.

RUNCITER: Yes. (*Nods*)

CHIP: Why the difference between your situation and ours?

RUNCITER: You want me to say?

CHIP: Yes.

RUNCITER: I'm not dead, Joe. The graffiti told the truth. You're all in cold-pac and I'm . . . (RUNCITER *pauses before continuing.*) . . . I'm sitting in a consultation lounge at the Beloved Brethren Moratorium. All of you are interwired, on my instructions; kept together as a group. I'm out here trying to reach you. That's where I am when I say "I'm outside:" that's why the manifestations, as you call them. For one week now I've been trying to get you all functioning in half-life, but—it isn't working. You're fading out one by one.

CHIP: What . . . what about Pat Conley?

RUNCITER: Yeah, she's with you, in half-life, interwired to the rest of the group.

CHIP: Are the regressions due to her talent? Or to the normal decay of half-life?

RUNCITER: (*With reluctance*) The normal decay. Ella experienced it. Everyone who enters half-life experiences it.

CHIP: You're lying to me, Glen.

RUNCITER: Joe, my god, I saved your life; I broke through to you enough just now to bring you back into full half-life functioning —you'll probably go on indefinitely now. If I hadn't been waiting here in this hotel room when you came crawling

Philip K. Dick

through that door, why hell—hey, look, goddam it; you'd be lying on that rundown bed dead as a doormat by now if it wasn't for me. I'm Glen Runciter; I'm your boss and I'm the one fighting to save all your lives—I'm the *only* one out here in the real world plugging for you. (RUNCITER *stares at* CHIP *with heated indignation and surprise, a bewildered, injured surprise, as if he cannot fathom what is happening.*) That girl, that Pat Conley, she would have killed you like she killed— (*He breaks off.*)

CHIP: Like she killed Wendy and Al, Edie Dorn, Fred Zafsky, and maybe by now Tito Apostos.

RUNCITER: This situation is very complex, Joe. It doesn't admit to simple answers.

CHIP: You don't *know* the answers. That's the problem. You *made up* the answers; you had to invent them to explain your presence here. All your presences here, your so-called manifestations.

RUNCITER: I don't call them that; I believe it was you and Al worked out that name. Don't blame me for what you two—

CHIP: You don't know any more than I do, about what's happening to us and who's attacking us. Glen, you can't say who we're up against because you don't know!

RUNCITER: I know I'm alive. I know I'm sitting out here in the consultation lounge at the moratorium.

CHIP: Your body in the coffin here at the Simple Shepherd Mortuary; did you look at it?

RUNCITER: No, but that really isn't . . .

CHIP: It had withered. Lost bulk like Wendy's and Al's and Edie's— and in a little while mine. Exactly the same for you: no better, no worse.

RUNCITER: In your case I got the Ubik. (*He pauses, scowling, chewing his lip gloomily.*) I got the Ubik.

CHIP: What is Ubik? (*There's no response from* RUNCITER.) You don't know that either. You don't know what it is or why it works. You don't even know where it comes from.

RUNCITER: (*After agonized pause*) You're right. Absolutely right. But I did want to save your life; that part is true. Hell, I'd like to save all your lives.

UBIK: The Screenplay

CHIP: We're in here and we can't do anything; you're sitting out there in the consultation lounge and you can't do anything.

RUNCITER: Correct, Joe.

CHIP: This may be cold-pac, but there is something more—something not natural to people in half-life. There are two forces at work, as Al and I figured out: one helping us and one destroying us. You're working with the force or entity or person that's trying to help us. You got the Ubik from them.

RUNCITER: Yes.

CHIP: So none of us know even yet who it is that's destroying us—or who it is that's protecting us; you think, though—

RUNCITER: I'm sure your enemy is Pat Conley.

CHIP: I almost agree. Almost.

RUNCITER: Pat Conley's chest was crushed. She died of shock and a collapsed lung, with multiple internal injuries, including a ruptured liver and a leg shattered in three places. Physically speaking, she's about four feet away from you; her body, I mean. So you see, I know a lot more than you.

CHIP: And we're all at the Beloved Brethren?

RUNCITER: With one exception: Sammy Mundo. He suffered massive brain damage and lapsed into a coma out of which they say he'll never emerge. The cortical—

CHIP: So Mundo is alive!

RUNCITER: I wouldn't call it "alive." They've run encephalograms on him; no cortical activity at all. A vegetable, nothing more. No personality, no motion, no consciousness—there's nothing happening in Mundo's brain, nothing in the slightest.

CHIP: So, therefore, you naturally didn't think to mention it.

RUNCITER: I mentioned it now. Mundo is at the Carl Jung Hospital, about a quarter mile from this moratorium.

CHIP: Rent a telepath from Ray Hollis. To read Mundo's mind. It would fit—he was disorganized and immature...a cruel, unformed, very peculiar personality. It would fit what we've been experiencing, this "pulling the wings off flies."

RUNCITER: We did that with Mundo; in brain-injury cases like this it's Standard Operating Procedure, to try to reach the person telepathically. No results; nothing. No frontal-lobe cerebration. Sorry, Joe.

40.

We see GLEN RUNCITER *seated in the consultation lounge of the Beloved Brethren Moratorium, a complex plastic disk attached to his ear, mike-tube bent near his lips; he is wearily removing this communications gear and getting heavily to his feet. He looks haggard, worn-out, and depressed. We hear once more the somber choral music piped throughout the moratorium: the Verdi "Requiem," this time the "Sanctus" section, at background level.*

RUNCITER: (*Into tube mike*) I'll talk to you later, Joe.

RUNCITER *stands stiffly, obviously having been seated for a very long time. We get a glimpse of the caskets of the half-lifers: several of them linked in series beyond a common glass wall. Closest half-lifer is badly mangled man—evidently* JOE CHIP's *corpse. Side door of lounge opens,* HERBERT SCHOENHEIT VON VOGELSANG *appears.*

HERBERT: Did you ring for me, Mister Runciter? Shall I put Mister Chip back with the others? You're done, sir?

RUNCITER: I'm done.

HERBERT: Did you—

RUNCITER: Yeah, I got through all right. We could hear each other fine this time.

HERBERT: The high-gain transduction coil we had installed—

RUNCITER: You should have used it from the start. (*Plodding from the lounge,* RUNCITER *comes to pay phone, puts in coin and dials.*) Len, I can't do any more today. I've spent the last twelve hours trying to get through to my people in cold-pac, and I'm exhausted. Would tomorrow be okay?

LEN NIGGLEMAN: (*Filter*) The sooner you file your official, formal deposition with us, the sooner we can begin civil action against Hollis. My legal department says it's open and shut; they're champing at the bit.

RUNCITER: They think they can make a civil charge stick?

LEN NIGGELMAN: (*Filter*) Civil and criminal. In the civil you'd get punative damages; in the criminal we'd get Hollis into the

UBIK: The Screenplay

slammer. The New York D.A. has already been—

RUNCITER: Tomorrow. After I get some sleep. This thing has damn near finished me off. My best people.

LEN NIGGELMAN: (*Filter*) Sure, Glen. Get a good night's sleep and then meet me in my office tomorrow, say at ten o'clock our time.

RUNCITER *rings off, wanders away from phone, seats himself even more wearily. As he rubs his eyes,* HERBERT *comes up.*

HERBERT: Can I provide you with anything, Mister Runciter? A cup of coffee? A twelve-hour amphetamine spansule? In my office I have a new stimulant which Geigy just put on the drug market; it'll—

RUNCITER: Flap away!

As HERBERT *departs,* RUNCITER *muses to himself.*

RUNCITER: (*Filter*) My best people. Especially Joe Chip. My organization—it's *gone*. God, where am I going to get trained inertials to replace those? And where am I going to find a field tester like Joe Chip? Why did I pick this place? Ella's here; you always return to what and where you know. Habit, coming here. It is, after all, the best; that's why she's here. I'll be here, too, someday. All of us. Like the Bible says, we all go to one place: the Beloved Brethren Moratorium in Zurich. (*Moment of respite in his thoughts. Then:*) Ella. I'd better talk to her again for a moment. Let her know how things are going. That's, after all, what I—

Getting to his feet, RUNCITER *starts in search of* HERBERT.

RUNCITER: (*Filter*) Am I going to get that damn thing, that Jory, this time? Or will I be able to keep her in focus long enough to tell her what Joe said? It's becoming so hard, with Jory growing and expanding and feeding on her and maybe on the others over there in half-life. The moratorium should do something about it; about him. Maybe they can't. Maybe there's never been anyone in half-life like Jory before . . . (*Slow fade*)

41.

"Andy Warhol" manifestation, very brief in duration; this time the spraycan label reads:

Philip K. Dick

> IT TAKES MAKES MORE THAN A BAG TO SEAL IN FOOD FLAVOR; IT TAKES UBIK PLASTIC WRAP— ACTUALLY FOUR LAYERS IN ONE. KEEPS FRESHNESS IN, AIR AND MOISTURE AND COLD OUT. WATCH THIS SIMULATED TEST.

Manifestation fades, and we see JOE CHIP's *dingy hotel room in Des Moines as before;* CHIP *is alone, startled to see door of room fly open.* DON DENNY *accompanied by middle-aged responsible-looking* DOCTOR *enter.*

DON DENNY: How are you, Joe? Why aren't you lying down? For chrissakes, get onto the bed!

DOCTOR: Please lie down, Mister Chip. (*Opens old-style black medical bag on vanity table.*) Is there discomfort along with the enervation and the difficult respiration? (DOCTOR *approaches bed with stethoscope.*)

Do you have any history of cardiac involvement, Mister Chip? Or your mother or father? (*Draws up wooden chair beside bed.*) Unbutton your shirt, please, or whatever that is you're wearing.

CHIP: I'm okay now.

DON DENNY: Let him listen to your heart.

CHIP: Runciter managed to get through to me. We're in cold-pac; he's on the other side trying to reach us. When you opened the door did you see Runciter?

DON DENNY: No.

CHIP: He was sitting in the chair across from me. Look on the vanity table and see if he left the spraycan of Ubik.

DENNY *does so, finds spraycan, holds it up and shakes it.*

DON DENNY: It seems empty.

CHIP: Almost empty. Spray what's left on yourself. Go ahead.

DOCTOR: Don't talk for a moment, Mister Chip.

DON DENNY: The others are dying, Joe.

CHIP: *All* of them?

DON DENNY: Everyone that's left.

CHIP: Pat, too?

DON DENNY: I found her on the second floor here. She seemed terribly surprised. Apparently she couldn't believe it, about her. I guess she thought she was doing it, with her talent. It must be a shock when you think—

CHIP: Why won't you use the Ubik?

DON DENNY: Hell, Joe; we're going to die. You know it and I know it. After I saw Pat's deterioration I went into the other rooms and that's when I saw the rest of them. That's why we took so long getting here; I had Doctor Taylor examine them. I couldn't believe they'd dwindle away so fast. The acceleration has been so—

CHIP: Use the Ubik or I'll use it on you.

DON DENNY: This is the end, isn't it? (DENNY *picks up Ubik can, points nozzle at himself.*) They're all dead; only you and I are left, and the Ubik is going to wear off in a few hours. And you won't be able to procure any more. Which will leave me.

DENNY *presses the button; shimmering vapor filled with particles of metallic light swirls about him. Rapidly,* DENNY *disappears within the nimbus. Both* DOCTOR *and* CHIP *watch; the cloud evaporates, but the person standing there is not* DON DENNY *any longer. Instead,* JOE CHIP *and we see an adolescent boy, mawkishly slender, with irregular button eyes beneath tangled brows. He wears an anachronistic white cotton drip-dry shirt, jeans and laceless leather loafers. On his overly elongated face is a misshapen smile, virtually a leer. No two features match: his straight hair, for instance, contradicts the interwoven bristles of his brows. His nose is too thin, too sharp, too long. We are perhaps reminded of the description given earlier by Shakespeare of Richard Third, including the almost hunchback stoop. The total impression is repellant and dreadful: an incomplete creature, which makes* CHIP *tremble.*

CHIP: Who are you?

The boy twitches, stammers as he responds.

JORY: Sometimes I call myself Matt and sometimes Bill. But mostly I'm Jory. That's my real name—Jory.

CHIP: Where's Denny? He never came into this room, did he?

JORY: I ate Denny a long time ago. Right at the beginning, before they came here from New York. First I ate Wendy Wright. Denny came second.

CHIP: What do you mean, "ate"?

JORY: I did what I do. It's hard to explain.

JORY *exhibits a mixture of pride, modesty and greed; it is revolting, especially because of the adolescent mannerisms.*

JORY: Anyhow, I've been doing it a long time to lots of half-life people. I eat their life, what remains of it. There's very little in each person, so I need a lot of them. I used to wait until they had been in half-life awhile, but now I have to have them immediately. If I'm going to be able to live myself. If you come close to me and listen—I'll hold my mouth open—you can hear their voices. Not all of them, but anyhow the last ones I ate. The ones *you* know.

With his grubby finger JORY *pokes at his upper left incisor, his head tilted on one side as he regards* CHIP, *waiting for his reaction.*

JORY: Don't you have anything to say?

CHIP: (*In a low voice*) It was you who started me dying down there in the lobby.

JORY: Me and not Patricia. I ate her out in the hall by the elevator, and then I ate what was left—the others. I thought you were dead. (JORY *rotates the spraycan of Ubik, scowling in a pimply way.*) I can't figure this out; what's in it? And, and—where does Runciter get it?

CHIP: *Mister* Runciter.

JORY: But Runciter can't be doing it; he's on the outside. This originates from within our environment—on this side of the glass. It has to, because nothing can come in from outside except words.

CHIP: So there's nothing you can do to me—you can't eat me because of the Ubik.

JORY: I can't eat you for a while. But the Ubik will wear off.

CHIP: You don't know that. You don't even know what it is or where it comes from.

CHIP: (*Filter*) I wonder if I can kill you. You are the thing that got Wendy. I'm seeing it face to face. I knew I eventually would. Al, the genuine Don Denny . . . the rest of them, of us. It even ate

IT TAKES MORE THAN A BAG TO SEAL IN FOOD FLAVOR: IT TAKES UBIK PLASTIC WRAP – ACTUALLY FOUR LAYERS IN ONE. KEEPS FRESHNESS IN, AIR AND MOISTURE AND COLD OUT. WATCH THIS SIMULATED TEST.

CHIP: Pat, too?

DON DENNY: I found her on the second floor here. She seemed terribly surprised. Apparently she couldn't believe it, about her. I guess she thought she was doing it, with her talent. It must be a shock when you think—

CHIP: Why won't you use the Ubik?

DON DENNY: Hell, Joe; we're going to die. You know it and I know it. After I saw Pat's deterioration I went into the other rooms and that's when I saw the rest of them. That's why we took so long getting here; I had Doctor Taylor examine them. I couldn't believe they'd dwindle away so fast. The acceleration has been so—

CHIP: Use the Ubik or I'll use it on you.

DON DENNY: This is the end, isn't it? (DENNY *picks up Ubik can, points nozzle at himself.*) They're all dead; only you and I are left, and the Ubik is going to wear off in a few hours. And you won't be able to procure any more. Which will leave me.

DENNY *presses the button; shimmering vapor filled with particles of metallic light swirls about him. Rapidly,* DENNY *disappears within the nimbus. Both* DOCTOR *and* CHIP *watch; the cloud evaporates, but the person standing there is not* DON DENNY *any longer. Instead,* JOE CHIP *and we see an adolescent boy, mawkishly slender, with irregular button eyes beneath tangled brows. He wears an anachronistic white cotton drip-dry shirt, jeans and laceless leather loafers. On his overly elongated face is a misshapen smile, virtually a leer. No two features match: his straight hair, for instance, contradicts the interwoven bristles of his brows. His nose is too thin, too sharp, too long. We are perhaps reminded of the description given earlier by Shakespeare of Richard Third, including the almost hunchback stoop. The total impression is repellant and dreadful: an incomplete creature, which makes* CHIP *tremble.*

CHIP: Who are you?

The boy twitches, stammers as he responds.

JORY: Sometimes I call myself Matt and sometimes Bill. But mostly I'm Jory. That's my real name—Jory.

CHIP: Where's Denny? He never came into this room, did he?

JORY: I ate Denny a long time ago. Right at the beginning, before they came here from New York. First I ate Wendy Wright. Denny came second.

CHIP: What do you mean, "ate"?

JORY: I did what I do. It's hard to explain.

JORY *exhibits a mixture of pride, modesty and greed; it is revolting, especially because of the adolescent mannerisms.*

JORY: Anyhow, I've been doing it a long time to lots of half-life people. I eat their life, what remains of it. There's very little in each person, so I need a lot of them. I used to wait until they had been in half-life awhile, but now I have to have them immediately. If I'm going to be able to live myself. If you come close to me and listen—I'll hold my mouth open—you can hear their voices. Not all of them, but anyhow the last ones I ate. The ones *you* know.

With his grubby finger JORY *pokes at his upper left incisor, his head tilted on one side as he regards* CHIP, *waiting for his reaction.*

JORY: Don't you have anything to say?

CHIP: (*In a low voice*) It was you who started me dying down there in the lobby.

JORY: Me and not Patricia. I ate her out in the hall by the elevator, and then I ate what was left—the others. I thought you were dead. (JORY *rotates the spraycan of Ubik, scowling in a pimply way.*) I can't figure this out; what's in it? And, and—where does Runciter get it?

CHIP: *Mister* Runciter.

JORY: But Runciter can't be doing it; he's on the outside. This originates from within our environment—on this side of the glass. It has to, because nothing can come in from outside except words.

CHIP: So there's nothing you can do to me—you can't eat me because of the Ubik.

JORY: I can't eat you for a while. But the Ubik will wear off.

CHIP: You don't know that. You don't even know what it is or where it comes from.

CHIP: (*Filter*) I wonder if I can kill you. You are the thing that got Wendy. I'm seeing it face to face. I knew I eventually would. Al, the genuine Don Denny . . . the rest of them, of us. It even ate

UBIK: The Screenplay

Glen Runciter's corpse as it lay in the casket at the mortuary; there must have been a flicker of residual protophasic activity in or near it, or something, anyhow, which attracted *this*.

DOCTOR: Mister Chip, I didn't have a chance yet to finish taking your blood pressure reading. Please lie back down.

CHIP: (*Astonished*) Didn't you see him— (*To* JORY) Didn't he see you change? Hasn't he heard what you've been saying?

JORY: Doctor Taylor is a product of my mind. Like every other fixture in this pseudo world.

CHIP: I don't believe it. (*To* DOCTOR) You heard what he's been saying, didn't you, doctor?

With a hollow whistling pop the DOCTOR *disappears.*

JORY: See?

CHIP: What are you going to do when I'm killed off? Will you keep on maintaining this 1939 world, this "pseudo world," as you call it?

JORY: Of course not; there's no reason to.

CHIP: Then it's all for me, just for me, this entire world.

JORY: It's not very large. One hotel in Des Moines. And a street outside the window with a few people and cars. I have the same cars and the same people and even the same buildings show up again and again; it's easier. I just produce the bare minimum I have to.

CHIP: You're not maintaining New York or Zurich or—

JORY: Why should I? No one's there. When you flew here from New York I had to create hundreds of miles of countryside—only I sort of, you know, cheated; did you notice it looked all the same? Even so I found it exhausting. I had to eat up a great deal to make up for that effort; in fact, that's the reason I had to finish off the others so soon after you got here—I was intending to save them longer. You're the one who's at fault.

CHIP: Why 1939? Why not our own contemporary—

JORY: I can't keep objects from regressing. Doing it alone, it was too much for me. I created 1992 at first, but then things began to, you know, deteriorate. The coins, the cream, the cigarettes— all those phenomena you noticed. And then Runciter—

CHIP: Mister Runciter.

JORY: ... kept breaking through from outside; that made it even harder for me. It would have been better if he hadn't interfered. (JORY *grins slyly.*) But I didn't worry; I knew you'd all figure it was Patricia; it would seem like her talent, like what it does. I thought maybe the rest of you would gang up and kill her. I would enjoy that, if that had worked out.

CHIP: What's the point of keeping this hotel and the street outside going for me, now that I know?

JORY: But I always do it this way.

CHIP: I'm going to kill you.

The fight between JORY *and* CHIP *begins with* CHIP *making the first move; he strikes at the larynx with his fist, to get it over with. The feeble neck however retreats; snarling* JORY *bites him. Great shovel teeth fasten deep into* CHIP*'s right hand; they hang on as, meanwhile,* JORY *raises his head lifting* CHIP*'s hand with his jaw.* JORY *stares at him unwinkingly.*

CHIP: (*Filter*) He's eating me!

CHIP: (*Aloud*) You can't. The Ubik keeps you away.

JORY: (*Teeth still sunk in* CHIP*'s hand*) Gahm grau.

JORY's *jaws work sideways like a sheep's, grinding* CHIP's *hand until the pain becomes too much.* CHIP *kicks* JORY. *The teeth release;* CHIP *steps backward, examining the blood rising from the punctures made by the teeth.*

CHIP: You can't do to me. What you did to them.

CHIP *grabs the spraycan of Ubik, points nozzle toward his bleeding wound. Weak stream of particles emerge; a fine film settles over the chewed tissue; as in a Biblical miracle, the wound instantly heals.*

JORY: And you can't kill me.

CHIP: Hell, I'm leaving.

CHIP *walks unsteadily to the door, opens it. Outside the long dingy hall;* CHIP *starts forward, being careful of his step. It seems real, though; the floor supports him. Camera follows him.*

JORY: Don't go too far. I don't keep too great an area going; like, if you were to get into one of those cars and drive—pretty soon

you'd reach a point where it, you know, breaks down. And you
wouldn't like that too much.

CHIP: I don't see what I have to lose.

CHIP *reaches elevator; presses button, waits.*

JORY: (*Calling after him*) I have trouble with elevators. They're complicated. Maybe you should take the stairs; that'd be less strain on us both.

Nodding, CHIP *does so; once more he is on stairs, but this time descending, and it is easy.*

CHIP: (*Filter*) Well, that's one of them. The destroyer that got all of us except for me. Behind Jory there is nothing; he—it—is the end. Will I meet the Other agency, who's protecting us? Probably not soon enough for it to matter. But I'd like to see it, too. Out of curiosity . . .

CHIP *reaches lobby, gazes around at the people and the great chandelier overhead. Just stands there; just looks. No thoughts on his part; he merely sees what we see, understands silently what we understand. Then walks slowly to main desk. For an interval he and* CHIEF CLERK *stand facing each other, as if both know something together which isn't spoken. Then at last* CHIP *speaks.*

CHIP: You have a restaurant that you'd recommend? Especially recommend, that's really good? Out of the ordinary?

CHIEF CLERK: Well, sir, there is the Matador. That's out of the ordinary.

Raises his hand to point direction.

CHIP: I'm lonely. Does the hotel have any source of supply? Any girls?

CHIEF CLERK: Not this hotel, sir. The Meremont does not pander.

CHIP: You maintain a good clean family hotel.

CHIEF CLERK: That is correct, sir.

CHIP: I was just testing you. I wanted to be sure what kind of hotel I was staying in.

Turning away, CHIP *crosses lobby to revolving front door; outside on the pavement he surveys all the 1930 style cars going past.*

CHIP: (*Filter*) How could Jory be so accurate—oh yeah; he was telling the truth. Decomposition back to these older forms is not his doing. They happened despite what he did. (CHIP *walks along sidewalk, hands in his pockets.*) These atavisms, re-emerging as Jory's strength wanes, they were always here, concealed within our world, ready to rise to the surface once again when something goes wrong. When the usual hand that steadies us slips somehow away—to disclose all this below. I guess this is why they say hell is below. Dim, and old, and below.

A square old Dodge taxi sputters past; CHIP *waves at it. Cab flounders noisily to the curb.*

CHIP: (*Filter*) Let's test Jory out, okay? Let's see what happens if I try to get away, far away, from here.

CHIP: (*Aloud, to taxi driver*) Take me for a ride through town. Go anywhere you want; I'd like to take the scenic route. (CHIP *climbs into back of cab.*) And after I've seen every street in Des Moines, drive me to the next town.

DRIVER: I don't go between towns, mister. But I'd be glad to drive you around the scenic part of Des Moines. It's a nice city, sir. You're from out of state, are you?

CHIP: From New York.

They drive along.

DRIVER: How do the folks feel about the war back in New York? Do you think we'll be getting into it? Roosevelt wants us—

CHIP: I don't care to discuss politics or the war. (*They drive in silence.*) Driver, are there any houses of prostitution here in Des Moines?

DRIVER: No.

We and CHIP *see a pretty girl walking along sidewalk, evidently window shopping; she has blond pigtails, an unbuttoned sweater over her print blouse, a bright red skirt and high-heeled shoes. He is at once interested; he peers at the girl, who looks to be in her early twenties.*

CHIP: Slow the cab. There, at the corner; stop.

DRIVER: She won't talk to you. She looks like a nice girl. In fact, she'll probably call for a cop.

CHIP: I don't care; stop anyhow. (*The old Dodge taxi bumbles its way to the curb, parking ahead of the slowly strolling blond-*

UBIK: The Screenplay

haired girl.) Hi, miss.

Girl regards him with curiosity; she has warm, intelligent blue eyes, which show no aversion or alarm. In fact she seems slightly amused, and in a friendly way.

GIRL: Yes?

CHIP: I'm going to die.

GIRL: Oh dear. Are you—

DRIVER: He's not sick. He's been asking after girls; he just wants a pick up.

GIRL *laughs, without hostility. Does not depart.*

CHIP: It's almost dinnertime. Let me take you to a good restaurant, like the Matador; I understand that's nice.

We see that CHIP *is trembling, as before, with both weariness and with cold; he rests his head on his arm, against the open window of the cab, as if finally giving up.*

GIRL: Are you all right?

CHIP: (*With effort*) I'm dying, miss. Like I said.

GIRL: Have the driver take you to the hospital.

CHIP: Can we have dinner together?

GIRL: Is that what you want to do? When you're—whatever it is. Sick? You are sick, then? Do you want me to take you to the hospital, is that it?

CHIP: To the Matador. We'll have braised fillet of Martian mole cricket; I mean . . . market steak. Beef. Meat of the cow. Do you like meat of the cow?

GIRL: (*She enters cab, beside* CHIP, *shuts door.*) He wants to go to the Matador, driver.

DRIVER: Okay, lady.

Taxi bumps out into traffic again; CHIP *remains resting against the open window, seemingly unaware, or virtually unaware, that the cab is in motion, or even that the* GIRL *is now there with him.*

GIRL: Care for a Lucky Strike? (*Extends pack to* CHIP, *touching him slightly, rousing him.*) "They're toasted," as the slogan goes. However, the famous phrase, "L.S.M.F.T.," won't come into existence until—

Philip K. Dick

CHIP: My name is Joe Chip.

GIRL: Yes.

CHIP: Do you like Des Moines? Lived here a long time?

GIRL: You sound very tired, Mister Chip.

CHIP: Oh hell. It doesn't matter.

GIRL: Yes it does (GIRL *studies him.*) Do you want me to tell you my name?

CHIP: (*Vaguely*) All parts of Des Moines look the same. Of course, Jory has to be economical—like he said—

GIRL: Well, I am not a deformation of Jory's. (*Opening her purse,* GIRL *rummages briskly within it.*) I'm not like *him.* (*Indicates the cab driver in the front seat.*)

Or like these little old dried-up stores and houses and this dingy street. All these juiceless people and their heolithic vehicles. Here, Mister Chip. (*From her purse she brings forth an envelope, which she passes to* CHIP.) This is for you. Open it now; I don't think either of us should have delayed so long.

Close up of CHIP's *fingers as he tears open the envelope; he seems more alert, now, more alive. In it he finds a stately, ornamented certificate. But neither he nor we can make out the printing; his hand is still shaking too much. However, it does resemble the "Andy Warhol" spraycan labels, and we do catch the word UBIK here and there, illuminated in mercurial colors like fire.*

CHIP: What's it say?

GIRL: From the company which manufactures Ubik. It's a guarantee, Mister Chip, for a free lifetime supply. Free because I know your psychological hangup regarding money—which isn't meant as a putdown; I regard it just as an idiosyncrasy. And a list, on the reverse, of all the drugstores which carry it. Two drugstores—and not abandoned ones—in Des Moines are listed. I suggest we go there first, before we have dinner. Here, driver. (GIRL *leans forward, hands the* DRIVER *a slip of paper—already written out!*)

Take us to this address. And hurry; they'll be closing soon. (*As cab picks up speed the* GIRL *sinks back beside* CHIP, *relaxing.*) We'll make it to the drugstore.

She pats CHIP's *arm reassuringly.*

CHIP: Who did you say you are?

GIRL-ELLA: My name is Ella. Ella Hyde Runciter. Your employer's wife.

CHIP: Glen's wife!

GIRL-ELLA: Yes, Joe. Right.

GIRL-ELLA *laughs a merry tinkly laugh, like the Good Fairy would be expected to; but also she is sexy enough and attractive enough to be more than a mere spirit, a mere wish-fulfillment mythic figure; she has slipped the unbuttoned sweater off, now, and we see her to be well-developed as a woman; she fills the print blouse charmingly. It is likely that* CHIP *is aware of this also.*

CHIP: On this side of the glass.

GIRL-ELLA: Pardon, Joe?

CHIP: You're here with us, in cold-pac.

GIRL-ELLA: I've been here a long time. Years, Joe. On this side.

CHIP: That's right. (*Nods*)

GIRL-ELLA: Fairly soon I'll be reborn into another womb, I'm pretty sure. At least, Glen says so. I keep dreaming about a smoky red light, and that's bad; that's not a morally proper womb to be born into.

She laughs a rich, warm laugh.

CHIP: Hey, you're the other one. Jory destroying us—you trying to help us.

GIRL-ELLA: "Trying" is the right word exactly. Trying and screwing up. Mostly anyway. Not always.

CHIP: Behind you there's no one?

GIRL-ELLA: Not that I know of.

CHIP: Just as there's no one behind Jory. I've reached the last entities involved.

GIRL-ELLA: I really don't think of myself as an "entity." I usually think of myself as Ella Runciter. Sometimes even as Ella Hyde, my maiden name. I even forget about that.

CHIP: But it's true.

GIRL-ELLA: Yes.

CHIP: Why are you working against Jory?

GIRL-ELLA: The troll has menaced me in the same way he's menaced you. We both know what he does. (*Her voice is firm, now. Intense.*) When I'm reborn, Glen won't be able to consult with me any longer. I want you to replace me. I want to know there is somebody Glen can come to and ask for advice and assistance from. You will be ideal. You'll be doing in half-life what you did in full-life.

CHIP: After you're reborn I won't succumb?

GIRL-ELLA: You have your lifetime supply of Ubik. As it says on the certificate I gave you.

CHIP: Maybe I can defeat Jory.

GIRL-ELLA: There are Jorys in every moratorium. This battle goes on wherever the dead face the living, wherever you have half-lifers. It's a verity of our kind of existence. It has to be fought on our side of the glass. By those of us actually in half-life, those that Jory preys on. Do you think you can do that? It'll be hard. Jory will be sapping your strength always, putting a burden on you that you'll feel as—the approach of death. Which is what it will be. Because in half-life we diminish constantly anyhow. Jory only speeds it up, the weariness and cooling-off that approaches anyhow. But then finally—the transition. To rebirth. So it's okay.

DRIVER: Here's your drugstore, lady.

GIRL-ELLA: I won't go in with you. I'll wait here.

CHIP *gets from cab, enters drugstore, which is much like the previous one we saw. A tall bald pharmacist wearing a formal vest and bow tie greets him at once, sharply.*

BALD DRUGGIST: Afraid we're closing, sir. I was just coming to lock the door.

CHIP: Well, I'm in. And I want to be waited on.

CHIP *hands the certificate which* ELLA *gave him to the* BALD DRUGGIST.

BALD DRUGGIST: "Ubik." I believe I'm out of that. Let me check and see.

CHIP: Jory.

BALD DRUGGIST: Sir?

UBIK: The Screenplay

CHIP: You're Jory. You invented this drugstore and everything in it. Except for the spraycan of Ubik. You have no authority over Ubik.

CHIP *himself heads toward display shelves, searching swiftly.*

BALD DRUGGIST: I've regressed all the Ubik in this store. (BALD DRUGGIST's *voice is now youthful, high-pitched:* JORY's *voice.*) Back to the liver and kidney balm. It's no good now.

CHIP: I'll go to the other drugstore that has it.

BALD DRUGGIST: (JORY's *voice: Lip synch*) It'll be closed.

CHIP: Tomorrow. I can hold out until tomorrow morning.

BALD DRUGGIST: (JORY's *voice: Lip synch*) You can't. And anyhow, the Ubik at that drugstore will be regressed too.

CHIP: Another town—

BALD DRUGGIST: (JORY's *voice: Lip synch*) Wherever you go it'll be regressed. Back to the salve or back to the powder or back to the elixir or back to the balm. You'll never see a spraycan of it, Joe Chip.

CHIP: (*With difficulty*) I can—bring it back to the present. To 1992.

BALD DRUGGIST: (JORY's *voice: Lip synch*) Can you, Mister Chip? (*Hands* CHIP *a square pasteboard container.*) Here you are, sir. Open it and you'll see—

CHIP: I know what I'll see. (*He removes carton, concentrating as he does so.*) Spraycan.

BALD DRUGGIST: (JORY's *voice: Lip synch*) It's not a spraycan, Mister Chip.

CHIP: You are a spraycan. This is 1992.

The BALD DRUGGIST *is turning out the lights in the drugstore one by one. The store sinks into darkness; the only source of light enters from the high street lamp outside.* BALD DRUGGIST *stands by front door, holds it open in mock politeness.*

BALD DRUGGIST: (JORY's *voice: Lip synch*) Come on, Mister Chip. Time to go home. She was wrong, was she not? And you won't see her much longer because she's so far on the road to being reborn that she's not thinking about you, not really. Not you or me or even Runciter. What Ella sees now are various lights: red and torpid, or maybe bright orange.

CHIP: (*Last try*) What I hold here is a spraycan!!

BALD DRUGGIST: (*Original own voice*) No. I'm sorry, Mister Chip. I really am. I wish we'd had it in stock for you, sir. Goodnight.

CHIP *sets the square pasteboard carton—still only half-opened—down on counter, turns, walks silently past* BALD DRUGGIST *and out of drugstore, onto evening sidewalk.*

CHIP: I think I'll send a complaint in writing to the manufacturer. About it. Your regressed goddam drugstore.

The old Dodge taxi is gone; CHIP *looks left and right, into the gloom. Several people, some with packages, sit on a bench; along comes a huge old clanking metal streetcar; the people rise and move out to meet it. One person remains seated on the bench, however. A woman.* CHIP *goes toward her, peering to see who it is. Is it* ELLA?

ELLA: Hi, Joe.

ELLA *rises; she appears—but it's so dark now—to be dressed differently: modern synthetic-leather coat possibly from our own era, very short skirt, chic hair style. Together,* ELLA *and* CHIP *walk along, among the dim shapes of evening, neither speaking for a while.*

CHIP: They—the drugstore was out of it.

ELLA: I know. I'm sorry. He was there inside waiting, wasn't he?

They continue on. Neon and incandescent lighting of stores are coming on, now. To their right they see a looming great entrance lit up with smoky red neon tubing reading: MATADOR. They halt.

CHIP: Don't go in there.

ELLA: (*Listlessly*) What difference does it make, Joe?

CHIP: A lot. Anyhow to me, anyhow.

ELLA: Let's go inside and get dinner. Isn't this the place you said was—

CHIP: Look at the color.

ELLA: (*Echoing him*) "The color"?

She glances, but still moves toward the red-framed entrance to "The Matador." The red light is unpleasant and harsh. Now we can see inside: smoky air, vague moving shapes. CHIP *approaches, and*

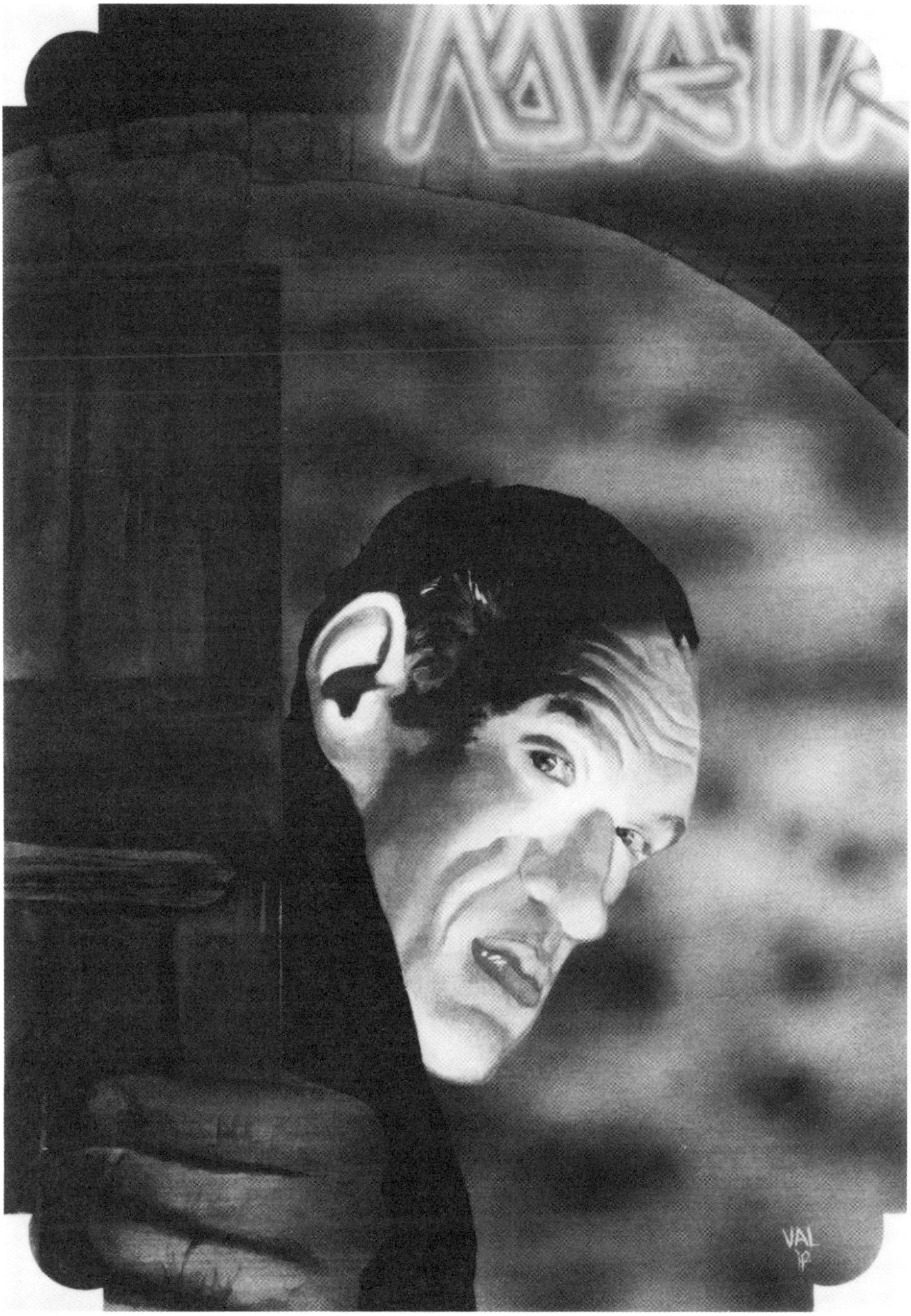
VAL

Philip K. Dick

the camera follows. We see inside better, now, as he sees: besides the tables with seated customers we can discern unmistakably the sight of some dreadful porno X-rated sex-act stage show in progress within; CHIP *draws back, revolted. Yet,* ELLA *continues to move very slowly, inevitably, toward the red-lit entrance.*

CHIP: This isn't the Matador.

ELLA: It says it is.

CHIP: (*Seizes her by the arm*) It's the smoky red light. The next womb—for you. A bad one.

Peering to see inside, intrigued, ELLA *pulls away.*

ELLA: What are they doing in there?

She cranes her neck to see; now she has almost passed across the entranceway and inside.

ELLA: Wow.

CHIP: Please don't. Wait.

ELLA: I'll see you, Joe.

ELLA *goes inside.* CHIP *hesitates in anguish mixed with aversion to the place. Anguish wins;* CHIP *follows after her. As he and* ELLA *pass through the red-lit entranceway a dreadfully ugly man inside, evidently an employee, grabs door and tugs it shut, after the two of them; the door slams violently and loudly in our faces; our last glimpse was not of* ELLA *and* CHIP *but of this great ugly troll, this huge dwarf wearing a narrow pin-stripe business suit, his lips painted and sensual, his eyes the black tombstone eyes associated with drug-use—that awful visage and the earbreaking thump of the door mix together; the sight seems almost to jolt the camera. That earbreaking thump on the soundtrack melds instantly into the drum strokes which open the "Dies Irae" section of the Verdi "Requiem." We see only swirling smoke, red neon fitful light, we hear only the overpowering sound of the music. It is the Day of Judgment, and* JOE CHIP *and* ELLA RUNCITER *are gone, behind the shut door.*

42.

The maternity wing of an extremely modern—in fact futuristic, which is to say, 1992—hospital. We have never been here before. GLEN RUNCITER *pacing in wide corridor, much like we saw him doing at the Beloved Brethren Moratorium. But he is not at the*

UBIK: The Screenplay

moratorium, although this maternity hospital wing resembles it. A white-clad doctor beckons RUNCITER, *who strides to recovery room. We see brief glimpse of young woman lying pale and inert in hospital bed; it is the pretty young pregnant* SECRETARY *of* HERBERT *at the Beloved Brethren Moratorium. But she does not bulge now; she has delivered her baby.*

Swift camera move as RUNCITER *confers with his own Runciter Associates employees, two of them in uniform, and then, to our surprise,* HERBERT *with several moratorium technicians who lug dollies of electronic equipment, consisting mostly of communications hardware. Then: Dissolve to* RUNCITER *in hospital corridor; he gazes through glass window (like glass wall separating him from the half-lifers in cold-pac) at incubators in which newborn babies can be seen. Sound track continues the Verdi "Requiem," and we hear only that, although* RUNCITER *and the others confer rapidly and repeatedly. Everything takes place here efficiently, as if long planned for—and well carried out, now that the time has come. There are no hitches;* RUNCITER *and his own Runciter Associates technicians and* HERBERT *and his moratorium technicians plus the hospital staff—all collaborate effectively. They bring the electronic communications equipment, which we are familiar with from the moratorium, toward the glass window behind which we see the newborn babies. It is obvious that* RUNCITER *is in charge of all this; it is his plan—so to speak, his "baby."*

43

RUNCITER *on this side of the glass, watching as, on the other side, the assorted professional technicians attach communications gear to one incubator in which one baby lies. Coils of wire carry a signal from the incubator to a booster; the signal is already being monitored by a technician wearing headphones; also, a tape recorder's drums are slowly turning. It is evident that they are attempting to pick up signals from this newborn baby. The technician wearing phones makes a gesture of glee; they've picked the signals up! Visibly,* RUNCITER *and* HERBERT *relax, grin. One would not know to look at the newborn baby that anything is happening inside its mind, but we can tell by the joy on the part of the adults that their project has worked out. Dials are adjusted, but it's all okay.* RUNCITER *moves away, rummages in his pockets for coins as he heads for pay phone. Stuffs coin into phone, begins to dial. But coin rolls back out of phone, rejected by it.* RUNCITER

Philip K. Dick

stuffs another coin in rapidly. Now music to background; we can hear his conversation.

RUNCITER: She's back. It went through—she went through—perfectly, and is right here with us.

However, as he talks, RUNCITER *frowns; he is staring down at the coin which the pay phone rejected. Abruptly close up of coin. We see profile on it of* JOE CHIP; *at same time we hear* RUNCITER *say wonderingly:*

RUNCITER: *Joe Chip* money? Yeah, yeah; it went perfectly.

Focus is still on the Joe Chip coin; it becomes freeze frame.

Final "Andy Warhol" manifestation of spraycan superimposition, with no sound track of any sort; there it hangs filling screen entirely; the label reads, but this time in roll-up sequence:

I AM UBIK. BEFORE THE UNIVERSE WAS, I AM. I MADE THE SUNS. I MADE THE WORLDS. I CREATED THE LIVES AND THE PLACES THEY INHABIT: I MOVE THEM HERE, I PUT THEM THERE. THEY GO AS I SAY, THEY DO AS I TELL THEM. I AM THE WORD AND MY NAME IS NEVER SPOKEN, THE NAME WHICH NO ONE KNOWS. I AM CALLED UBIK, BUT THAT IS NOT MY NAME. I AM. I SHALL ALWAYS BE.

Fade out.

UBIK: THE SCREENPLAY
by Philip K. Dick

illustrated by Doug Rice, Val Lakey-Lindahn, and Ron Lindahn

The text was set in Century Book by Virgo Graphics, Oak Park, Illinois. The introduction and foreword were set by Great Faces, Minneapolis, Minnesota. This book was printed and bound by Braun-Brumfield, Inc., Ann Arbor, Michigan. The text paper is a 60# acid-free stock with extended shelf life.

Fifty copies of this book were printed on 70# Mohawk Superfine paper, bound into leather and boxed. They are signed by the artists and by the authors of the introduction and foreword. Philip K. Dick's signature, clipped from checks and provided by his estate, was tipped into each of those copies. These fifty copies make up the Special Edition of the screenplay.

The book was designed by Rhip Thornhill and Ira M. Thornhill, with assistance by Robert T. Garcia and Luke McGuff.

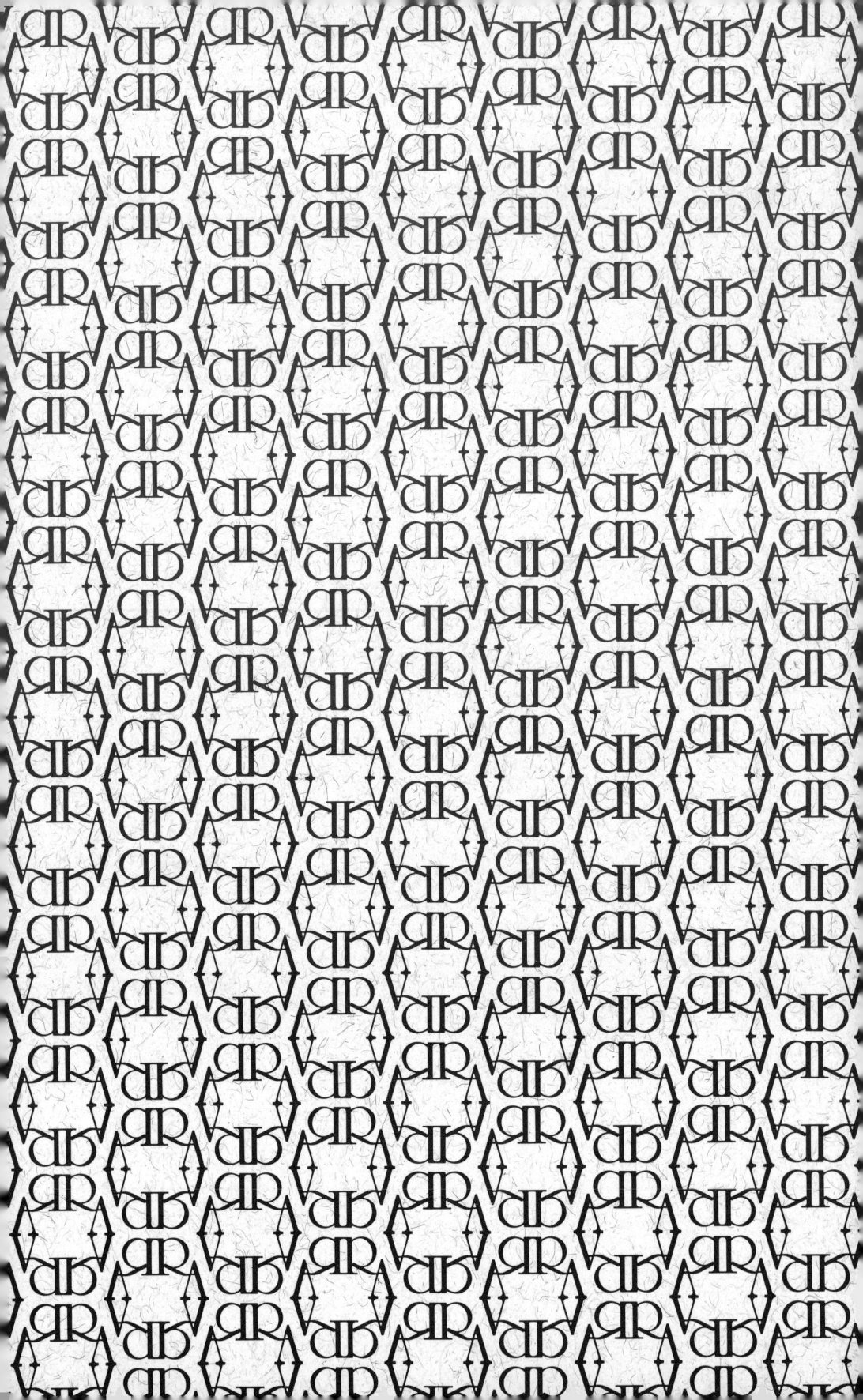